AMERICAN CLASSICS

COLONIAL
DAYS AND WAYS

As Gathered from Family Papers

HELEN EVERTSON SMITH

FREDERICK UNGAR PUBLISHING CO.
NEW YORK

Republished 1966 in the
AMERICAN CLASSICS SERIES

Reprinted from the edition of 1900

Decorations from original edition by
T. GUERNSEY MOORE

Printed in the United States of America

Library of Congress Catalog Card No. 65-29075

CONTENTS

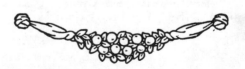

CHAPTER I

THE ALPHABET OF COLONIAL STUDY

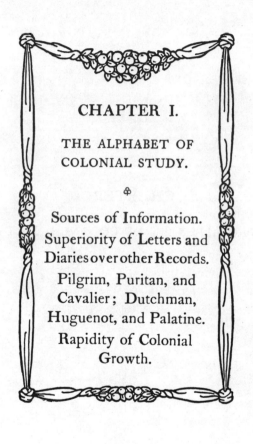

CHAPTER I.

THE ALPHABET OF COLONIAL STUDY.

&

Sources of Information.
Superiority of Letters and
Diaries over other Records.
Pilgrim, Puritan, and
Cavalier; Dutchman,
Huguenot, and Palatine.
Rapidity of Colonial
Growth.

WITH the gathering of relics to make suitable exhibits at the centennial celebration of our national independence, there came a general awakening of interest in all things pertaining to the history of our Revolutionary War and of the few years preceding it. Beginning with an interest only in this special period, the slow fire spread backward until now there are few persons —at least, of English, Dutch, Huguenot, or even of the late-coming Palatine descent — who are not increasingly interested in all that pertains to the earliest colonists. Especially is this true — probably because reliable information concerning it is so difficult of access — in whatever pertains to the home life, the employments, the enjoyments, the hardships, and the habits of our ancestors in those far-away days when the comforts and conveniences which they possessed were, as compared with our own, proportionately as those of the Indians when compared with those of the English in 1620.

So far, it must be confessed that, while the amount of information painfully gathered from town records, wills, inventories, letters, traditions, and relics is not inconsiderable, we are not as greatly the gainers by it all as we should be. We have the alphabet, but we do not yet know how to make words, still less how to construct the sentences, which shall tell us the true story of the most interesting beginning which any people has ever had.

Our national life has not been one of growth from savagery up, through many wars, through centuries of depression and oppression, of slow disintegrations and slower constructions, but is the result of deliberate purpose on the part of the majority of the first colonists, of no matter what creed or nationality, to occupy this wide, wild, new land, free to the first comer, and bring to it all the best of the institutions of the Old World, while leaving behind all that was worn out, all that had served its day.

For this reason, if for no other, the smallest traces of our national beginnings should be sought for; but not as one gathers pebbles on the seashore, to bring them home, turn them over, and throw them away. Every old record, every homely detail, every scrap of old furniture, every bit of home handicraft, above all, every familiar old letter or diary or expense-book, should be treasured; not always each for its own sake, but because each thing, however valueless by itself, is a letter in our alphabet, and, when read in connection with something else, may help in the formation of a word hitherto unknown to us.

In forming pictures of home life in the colonies, dates, places, and social classes must all be most carefully considered. Slow-moving as those pre-electric days now seem to us, there yet was a constant and, when rationally considered, a rapid progression, from the moment of the first landing at Jamestown onward.

The life conditions which prevailed in the New England colonies from 1620 to 1640 were by no means the same as those which prevailed in the same colonies during the next two decades, and in the other colonies they were at no time quite the same as in New England. The settlers of Virginia, Delaware, and Maryland were not of the same creeds, either political or religious, as those which prevailed in New England. They had more money, not having been obliged to make their flitting under such adverse circumstances, and climate had also its influence.

The Dutch held very similar religious and political views to those of the New England colonists, but their commercial instincts were stronger, their aggressiveness was less vehement, and their love of home comforts and knowledge of how to obtain them were much greater, for during the fifteenth and sixteenth centuries Holland was at the head of the commerce and manufactures of the world. Besides this, many of the immigrant Hollanders were either wealthy themselves, or were the well-provided offshoots from wealthy families who were disposed to enlarge their estates by commerce in the new lands.

The first three sets of colonists had passed through their pioneer stages, and gathered around themselves a fair degree of all the accompaniments of civilization before the advent of the fourth distinct and considerable body of settlers. These were the refugee Huguenots. In religion the Huguenots were as Calvinistic in their creed as were the Puritans and the Dutch, and were fully as earnest and steadfast in their belief, while the persecutions which the Puritans had suffered in England could no more be compared with those which had been endured for nearly two centuries by the Huguenots than the privations of one of our late Spanish captives could be compared with the sufferings of the colonists harried by the Indians in the seventeenth and eighteenth centuries.

Whether they had been rich or poor in France, there were very few of the Huguenot refugees who were not in the depths of poverty when they reached here. But they were gentle (in both senses of the word), they were trained in many arts, and they had the keen perceptions, the courtesy, and the easy adaptability of their race. Home life among them was different from that of any of the other colonists, partly because they had the advantage of coming to a land which had already been occupied for more than threescore years by laborious, progressive, and intelligent settlers, and partly because they came from a land which was in some things more advanced than either Holland or England. Politically the Huguenots had little sympathy with either English or Dutch. Their race was strongly monarchical by instinct; the rights of the individual man had never assumed their proper proportions in the eyes of Frenchmen.

The last of the great immigrations was that of the Palatines. In modern times there never has been such wholesale abandonment of home and fatherland as that by these unfortunate members of a home-loving race, driven by scores of thousands forth from the land of their birth by unendurable misery. Their home had been the battleground of Europe. Great kings and petty princes, Catholics and Protestants, had alike fought over it, burned its villages, destroyed its crops, leveled its strongholds, and harried its people until they had no hope remaining. In sheer desperation they begged from the compassion of England a passage to and a home in the wilds of the new land. Theirs is a history as yet inadequately written, but it is worthy of the pen of a really good historian, and when one shall arise from among their descendants theirs will prove to be a worthy and in some respects an unexampled record.

In studying the lives of the early colonists these different origins should always be considered.

The one colony must not be judged by another. The Puritan,— a political as well as a religious exile,— persecuted for his political views even more than his religious tenets, came here to found an empire where all his views should have room and liberty to expand. He was keen-witted, and,— *for his day*, be it ever understood,— in spite of his rigid notions of morality, and of all modern assertions to the contrary, he was no narrower in his strictness than was the roistering Cavalier in his laxity of morals. The harshness of the Puritan toward those who disagreed with him was tenderness and mercy compared to the "justice" meted out to either religious or political dissidents in old England, or, for that matter, in any other country in Europe, with the possible exception of Holland, at that period. Neither man nor nation should be judged by other than the standards of his time.

The conditions of the Puritan's life were hard, but full of mental, moral, and physical health. Whether gentle or simple, he despised no handicraft, neglected no means of cultivation, shirked no duty (nor did he permit any other to do so, if he could help it), and he fought his way upward, unhasting, unresting.

The settlers of the fertile Southlands were also principally of English blood, yet they differed widely from those of the sterile North. They were courageous, of course. A minority came under compulsion, but the majority came of their own free will, and cowards did not cross the ocean in those days, when the sea and the wilderness had real terrors for even the boldest. The love of liberty was in their blood, and both the traditions of their past and the comparatively genial conditions by which they were surrounded gave them easy and comfortable views. If the Englishman of the North were strenuous, energetic, a warm friend and a stern foe, he of the South was strong, generous, and joyous. If each were disposed to look a little askance at the other when the world went well with both, when trouble threatened either the fraternal blood flowed warm and true. We are all proud of them both — stern Puritan, gay Cavalier.

The Dutchman was milder than the Puritan, but every way as stiff-necked, and was an inborn republican as well as an educated Calvinist. Slower in his perceptions, narrower in his conceptions, and more prejudiced than even the Puritan, his faults were not so glaring because less aggressive, and the strength of his friendships and family affections hid them from the view of those who lived nearest him. As a mariner and as a trader, as well as in the arts which tend to make life easier and more comfortable, he had few equals, and our country owes much of its subsequent prosperity to the Dutchman's commercial and industrial instincts. We are ever grateful to him.

The Huguenot was devout, unambitious, affectionate of heart, artistic, cultivated, adaptable. He brought to us the arts, accomplishments, and graces of the highest civilization then known, together with a sweet cheerfulness all his own. Not a colony or a class but was ameliorated by his influence, and, consciously or unconsciously, we all love him.

The Palatine came to our shores desperate with misery. Although Protestant, his faith was not Calvinistic, neither did it fill so large a place in his thoughts. To the older colonists he seemed to be material, almost sordid, in his aims; but they understood neither his language nor his desperation. Perhaps they did not sufficiently try to do so. So he was left to himself, and so difficult was he of assimilation that even to-day those of his descendants who live a little off from the highways of commerce may still be found speaking but very imperfect English, if any, and living in self-centered communities, with little heed of the outside world, shut off from its influence. Industrious, frugal, unprogressive, living for himself alone, we still do not comprehend him.

Now, it is certain, from the nature of things, that the home lives of all these different bands of colonists must have differed widely. None had luxuries and few had comforts, as we now understand these terms, but each had some possessions, some ways, some deficiencies, and some attainments which belonged to none of the others; hence it is that a knowledge of the home life and personal characteristics prevalent in one colony does not imply a knowledge of those of another.

Even the details of domestic life differed somewhat in all the colonies, and a thing sometimes forgotten is that the house furnishings and personal habits, as well as the degrees of mental culture, differ with every advancing decade. Improved conditions came with a rapidity that was unexampled until that time. Because the first New England immigrants were obliged to live in moss-chinked and mud-plastered log huts, it does not follow that they long continued to live in them. In fact, it was but a few years before very substantial and comfortable dwellings were erected by the better class in all the colonies. The " Old Stone House " of Guilford, Connecticut, erected in 1639, is still an exceedingly comfortable and even handsome residence, though it has been damaged by some ill-judged alterations for which there was no excuse, because they have in no way added to the convenience or comfort of the inmates.

Two or three years later than the building of the Guilford house, there was erected in Hartford, Connecticut, a two-story house of squared timbers, covered with overlapping shingles on the sides, for the Rev. Thomas Hooker. Of this house a cut is given in Barbour's " Historical Collections of Connecticut," which shows it to have been not only a substantial, but, though a simple, yet a noticeable mansion for that period in the old England as well as in the New. The house erected for Mr. William Whiting about the same time is said to have been still better. The house furnishings of Mr. Hooker and Mr. Whiting, as inventoried after their deaths, would not seem very plentiful or luxurious to-day, but, read in connection with the similar inventories of the same date belonging to the yeoman or petty gentry classes in England, do not show many marked differences. Even when compared with the inventories of the larger landed proprietors in England, there is not much to choose in the way of comforts, though undoubtedly there is in that of articles of luxury and display. In these there is as much difference between the possessions of Mr. Hooker and Mr. William Whiting of Hartford and those of an English gentleman of high social grade, as there is between an English nobleman's belongings and those of a Frenchman of similar rank, or those of a Hollander of the rich merchant class at the same period. To the French nobleman or the untitled but wealthy Dutchman, the interior of the English nobleman's castle must have seemed to the full as barren of beauty and of comfort as the homes of the Hartford settlers would have seemed to all of them.

A few years later than the deaths of Mr. Hooker and Mr. Whiting, the recorded inventories grow longer and fuller. Stools gradually disappear from them and chairs are increasingly in evidence. Forks are not named until well on to the opening of the seventeenth century, and then they are of silver, and are first mentioned in the will of a citizen of Boston in the last quarter of the seventeenth century, at about which time they seem to have come into use among the upper classes in England, having been introduced there from France and Holland.

It may be taken for granted that the wealthiest settlers of New England in 1630 were a little better off in comforts than the poorest of 1650, and so on. The advance was continuous. So much industry, intelligence, energy, and invention were applied to the work that the progress was marvelous.

The same process was going on in all the colonies. The Dutchman, when he became an English subject, did not change his character or his ways, but his growth was steady, if, perhaps, a trifle slower than that of his English neighbor. It must be remembered that he started from a higher plane of comfort (Holland being much in advance of England in this regard), so that by the middle of the eighteenth century both stood upon about the same level in these things. In the meanwhile, both had been greatly helped by the incoming of the artistic, polished, and thrifty French element. The latter brought but few articles of luxury or even of utility, for, like the persecuted Armenians who lately sought our shores, the dangers and difficulties of their escape made such importations impossible; but they brought the manufacturing

and decorative skill to supply all deficiencies, and
also the power and the will to impart their skill,
and a few of them, like the Jays of Bedford, had
been able to send some of their wealth to this
country in advance of their own emigration. Very
little of all that was left behind was ever regained.

As sources of knowledge concerning household
possessions of the colonists, wills and the inventories
accompanying them have been too much relied
upon — not because they are not accurate, for this,
of course, they are, but because they do not cover
ground enough. As a rule, the larger the estate
the less likely was there to be an inventory of
household possessions, their appraisement and division among heirs being usually made by agreement.
In several distinct lines of colonial families which
I have traced back through seven and eight generations to the years beginning with 1630, I have discovered comparatively few wills, and, after about
1650, these were seldom accompanied by inventories of household possessions. Even when an
estate had been administered upon, in ordinary
cases the more purely personal property had apparently been divided by lot or private agreement,
without public appraisal. Especially is this found
to be the case in families numbering lawyers among
its members. In such families, when wills were
made, some person was nearly always named as
residuary legatee, in order, probably, to prevent
the necessity for giving detailed information of

such purely private matters to a curious local public.

From the extent and variety of my researches in this line, I have come to have little doubt that this aversion to recorded inventories of household possessions was stronger in proportion to the wealth of the deceased. Hence it is unfair to suppose that the inventories which remain give accurate ideas of the kinds and qualities of the household furnishings of all the classes in a colony.

Perhaps it is due to too great a reliance upon such sources of information that many persons are in the habit of thinking that our ancestors possessed only the plainest, most uncouth, and most comfortless of furnishings. This was quite true of even the wealthy among the first comers, but it speedily ceased to be true even of those who were not wealthy. The first immigrants among the Puritans had not a floor carpet among their possessions; but the number used in England in the first half of the seventeenth century was small, and they were considered quite in the light of effeminate luxuries. By 1660, or a little later, the always ugly and hard-to-be-swept, but all-enduring (and much-inflicting) rag carpet came into use, while those of the better class were usually provided with several of the excellent and easily swept but equally ugly yarn carpets, which could be and were made in those private families who were rich enough to provide the material, own the looms, and pay for the weaving. A few fine carpets were imported from the Netherlands, but only by the wealthiest colonists. By the middle of the eighteenth century, the yarn carpets were made and sold by village weavers, and had thus become comparatively plentiful. I find no evidence that rag carpets were used in the better sort of houses, except in rear passages and inferior rooms. Not long ago it was desired to restore one of the living-rooms in the most venerated house in North America to its condition in the years between 1776 and 1800, and preparations were made by one of our patriotic societies to cover its floor with a rag carpet. This seems an error in judgment. As Washington imported most of the finer clothes for himself and his immediate family, as well as their rich bed-hangings, their handsomest articles of furniture, and the best of wines for his family consumption, it is hardly likely that he did not follow the fashion of other gentlemen of his social rank, and import carpets for his best rooms, while using those of woven yarn for all inferior purposes.

At one time there was a general impression that all the immigrant families of good standing had brought over with them many rich articles of furniture, much silver plate, and even many articles of porcelain. Later on it had to be acknowledged that nothing but the most essential of household furnishings could have been permitted on vessels which were already entirely overcrowded with pas-

sengers and the animals which were essential to life
and agriculture in the new land, while " *Mayflower*
tea-pots " became a laughing-stock when it was remembered that tea did not come into use in Great
Britain until many years after the landing of the
Pilgrims.

After this there set in a reaction, and now the
pendulum has swung almost as far the other way.
While it is true that fine furnishings were the exception in the colonies as long as they continued
to be such, it is untrue that there were not many
families well supplied with all the comforts and
luxuries that were usual in families of similar rank
in old England. There is now in the possession
of a descendant of the original owner, and in perfect
preservation, a handsomely inlaid mahogany sideboard of the sort known as Chippendale, which
was imported by a Connecticut farmer in 1737, at a
cost, including that of transportation, of thirty-nine
pounds fifteen shillings sterling, as witnessed by
the time-yellowed receipted bill of the shipper,
which is still preserved. This cannot have been
an isolated instance, yet we are now asked to believe
that the stern conditions in the first half-century in
the colonies prevailed until after the colonial period
had passed by.

The second error is as great as the first. The
colonial stage of our existence was one of continual
advancement. The colonists were of different
races, of different social grades, of differing stages

of intellectual growth, of varying degrees of wealth ;
hence they cannot be judged by inflexible standards, and colonial life should be carefully studied,
almost as scholars study the history of ancient
Nineveh and Babylon. From the scanty fragments
of a long-neglected past we may gather our alphabet and learn to construct our sentences aright.

CHAPTER II

THE CONTENTS OF AN ANCIENT GARRET

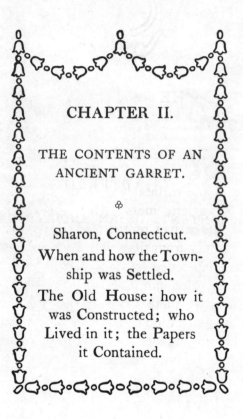

CHAPTER II.

THE CONTENTS OF AN ANCIENT GARRET.

☙

Sharon, Connecticut.
When and how the Town-
ship was Settled.
The Old House: how it
was Constructed; who
Lived in it; the Papers
it Contained.

THE beautiful village of Sharon, lying picturesquely along one of the broad natural terraces which form the western slopes of the southern spurs of the Berkshire Hills, was not one of the earliest settlements of Connecticut. A few stragglers, mostly from the banks of the Hudson River, had reared their temporary homes in this vicinity from time to time, but these had for the most part faded away when the township was laid out, in 1733, and it was not until several years after this that there were enough inhabitants to justify an application to the Assembly for an act of incorporation. Hence it would hardly be expected that papers relating to the very earliest colonial periods should be found here. But the first settlers of Sharon were not fresh immigrants from the Old World; they were all, or nearly all, descended from the pioneer colonists of New England, and naturally brought with them some of the relics and records that their parents and grandparents had accumulated.

In Sharon, among several fine houses of late

19

colonial dates, is one in which, during more than a hundred and thirty years, six generations of one family have lived quiet and happy but full and not uninteresting lives.

In the wide and lofty garrets of this house are stored many thousands of letters and other papers such as generations of cultivated and undestructive persons would naturally accumulate around them. Some of these papers are packed in oaken chests which had brought household plenishings "across the water" in the early days of the seventeenth century; some are in other chests of cherry wood, which were probably made in this country in the first decades of the colonial period; some are in the hair-covered, brass-nailed, and round-topped trunks of a later day; some are discovered packed in bandboxes which may once have contained elaborate periwigs, or immense and costly Leghorn bonnets; and again we find papers, valuable or useless, as the case may be, tucked away under the eaves in old baskets of Indian make, or in open pine-wood boxes, and even in barrels.

Some years ago, Mrs. E. P. Terhune (Marion Harland) visited this old house, and in her valuable and altogether charming book concerning "Some Colonial Homesteads and their Stories" has mentioned the old garret and its papers. She says:

"We climb the stairs to the great garret. A large, round window, like an eye, is set in a gable; the roof slopes above a vast space, where the towns-

people used to congregate for dance and speech-
making and church 'entertainments' before a public hall was built; . . . and in the middle of the
dusky spaciousness, a long, long table over which
is cast a white cloth. . . . Family papers! . . .
Hampers, corded boxes, and trunks full of them!
The hopes, the dreads, the loves, the lives of nine
generations of one blood and name." But the last
clause is hardly correct. The nine generations
who are represented here are of several names and
even of differing nationalities; but the blood of
them all is mingled in the veins of their descendants, the present owners of the old house.

During all the years that these old papers were
accumulating they were carefully dusted once or
twice a year, but not always replaced in their various receptacles with the reverential care which
they deserved. Indeed, it is known that during
the dozen years or so which succeeded 1845, servants who had neglected to provide kindlings for
the fires were occasionally permitted to use the
garret's store of papers for their purpose. Notwithstanding this culpable carelessness, great quantities still remained at the time that my interest in
them was first aroused, now a great many years
ago. From these papers the larger part of the
materials for the following chapters has been culled,
though some of the things that are here related are
on the authority of family traditions, notes of which
I began taking when I was eleven years old, as I

heard them narrated by parents, grandparents, and great-uncles and -aunts. These notes I continued to take at intervals for about eighteen years, by the end of which time many of the beloved narrators had gone to rejoin those whom they had held in such faithful and affectionate remembrance. Whenever anything is told on the authority of traditions only, it is thus expressly stated; but most of the information is from the abundant store of written sources.

The house in which the before-mentioned papers had been preserved is a fine specimen of the best period of our colonial architecture. The part which is now a capacious wing, running back from the main structure, was the first to be erected, and was reared on the foundations of a still earlier building. This first portion of the new home was completed about 1765 and was in itself a spacious dwelling. The cellars and kitchen were in its basement, and a very large dining-hall, with two other good-sized rooms, were on its first floor. These were flanked by piazzas (or rather *stoeps*) on the north and south sides. The wing's bedrooms were on the second floor, with windows in the long, sloping roof, whose peak was filled by a garret of good dimensions.

In this broad and comfortable dwelling, the owner, Simeon Smith, M.D., lived with his family while the very much larger main house was in the process of construction. And a slow process it was in those laborious days! Just when the wing was begun we do not know, but as it is of the same well-cut stone as the main house, which was not finished until some time during the Revolutionary War, we may hardly credit it with consuming much less than three years. There were then no steam-drills to assist in cutting the finely fitted stones. Water-power sawmills existed in this region at the time, and such planks as were used in the building were mostly sawed by them; but all the heavy timbers — and very heavy they are — appear to have been hewn with the carpenter's broadax, while the matchings of the floor-boards were all cut by hand.

The walls of both the wing and the main house were very solidly built of deftly fitted stones, laid with a fine regard for shape and color, and are from sixteen inches to two feet in thickness. The windows are surrounded by ornamental settings of red brick, which are of an unusually large size. The rear wall of the main house was built up against the exterior of the western gable of the wing, and the two walls thus joined are fifty-two inches thick where a large doorway connects the two structures. It is said that the foundations of the main house were begun before the completion of the walls of the wing, and were allowed to stand through the frosts of several successive winters " so that they might be well settled." The whole work was under the direction of a Genoese architect, who is stated to have been a political exile, and who brought some of his countrymen as assistants. The mortar he used is to-day as firm as the stone it cements, and is the admiration of modern architects and masons. I have often heard my grandfather say that his great-uncle, for whom the house was built, had told him that the Genoese was so jealous lest some one should discover the secret of this mortar that he set guards and took other precautions to keep away all intruders while he was mixing it. Probably the secret of its enduring quality is in the fact that very finely powdered stone and brick were used in the place of sand. With the purely manual labor of those days, this alone would have made the building a slow affair.

The foundations being considered sufficiently settled, the superstructure of the main building began to rise in 1773, and was roofed and its walls plastered by the opening of the campaign of 1775. From this time onward there was little thought to bestow upon so personal a matter as the building of a dwelling-house. Country-building was a much more important business.

In the early summer of 1775, the widowed Mrs. Samuel Smith, formerly of Suffield, Connecticut, and then living with her youngest son, Simeon, saw her second son, the Rev. Cotton Mather Smith, depart as chaplain to Colonel Hinman's regiment, in General Schuyler's army at Ticonderoga, where he remained until incapacitated for further duty by the camp-fever. A year later the old lady bade a Spartan mother's God-speed to her son, Dr. Simeon Smith, who, as captain of a company of Sharon men, equipped largely at his own expense, joined the troops under General Washington's immediate command, enduring all the hardships and misfortunes of the Long Island campaign. What was house-building compared to such work as this — even the erection of a house originally intended to have been one of the finest in New England? Its owner worked for and believed in better days to come, and did not relinquish his plans; but they were necessarily slow in fulfilment, and the main house, though occupied in 1777 and onward, was not fully finished until after the peace, and even then not entirely in consonance with the original designs.

From this date onward until about 1830 the great garret, which spreads over the entire main house, was frequently used as a substitute for a public hall. In it school exhibitions and examinations were held twice yearly, and for every form of village entertainment which was esteemed to be too high in its aims to be fittingly placed in the tavern, or too secular for the church, the lofty and spacious garret was generously offered. Decorated with evergreens and home-made flags, it made a pleasing and commodious place for social gatherings.

Probably even at this time papers had begun to accumulate in the spaces under the steep slopes of the hipped roof between the dormer-windows along the sides and ends of the old garret; for, in 1788, Dr. Smith, writing from Vermont, requests his nephew to "Look in the big cedar chest which Mother brought from Suffield, and which stands at the very south end of my big Garret, and you will find there the deeds of the Judge Badcock farm which I wish to have sent to me by some safe hand."

The mass of papers remaining here include many thousands of letters, several diaries, a great number of legal documents of both public and private natures, as well as piles of antiquated ledgers, bound, for the most part, in a sort of undressed leather, and big enough to have required an entire sheepskin for each tome. This mass of unassorted papers spreads over all the years, from the landings of the earlier immigrants in Massachusetts and Connecticut, down to near the middle of the present century. Naturally, the number of documents that have survived from the hundred years beginning with 1636 is not as large as we would wish; but from about 1730 the number began to increase, and from 1754 onward the material — though often leaving gaps just where they are most unwelcome — is remarkably abundant.

From these sources I have drawn what I believe to be, though incomplete, yet, as far as they extend, faithful pictures of the home life of the better class of persons in several places and periods of our colonial existence.

Such information as we may gather from town and church records is invaluable in its way; but from such sources we need not expect to get any but the scantiest glimpses of the home life. We now have daily newspapers and society journals to chronicle public and private events, and they certainly tell a great deal about the daily life of all classes among us; yet if, two centuries hence, these things should be the only testimony that had survived, can we conceive that our homes might be justly pictured from them? Or should we fare any better if judged by the records of the law-courts? Yet these would be riches compared with the meager sources which have come to us from colonial days. Concerning the homes and home life of the colonists our best materials must come from the comparatively few traditions that were committed to paper long enough ago to be granted a measure of authenticity, and from the relatively few contemporary family papers which have escaped from the inevitable losses by fires, removals, and — worst of all — the destruction by the Gallios who "cared for none of these things," until a tardily awakened interest in our ancestry has caused many of the heedless transgressors to remember and shudder at the bonfires fed by such unprized but now priceless material.

This little book relates what I have patiently gleaned concerning the home life of a few fairly representative families in the colonies of New York and Connecticut. These families were originally of several nationalities — English, Dutch, Scotch, and French Huguenots; yet, in the course of generations, all became related. Papers once belonging to or concerning each one of them, some of them unknown to each other even by name until long years after the papers were written, and some of them never so known, have long been lying side by side in the silent garret, and the descendants of the writers of most of the diaries and correspondence may now be found scattered from the Atlantic to the Pacific and from Canada to the Gulf.

In the earliest of these papers we find evidence of great privations heroically endured — not from hope of worldly advantage, but from the highest of motives. The gently born and bred, the conscientious laborer, the strictest Puritan, the Scotch Presbyterian, the sturdy Dutch Calvinist, and the patient Huguenot were all alike upheld by their sturdy faith in God and righteousness. They made mistakes enough, all of them — the Puritan perhaps more than the rest, because he was Anglo-Saxon, and therefore could never imagine himself to be in the wrong about any matter, and, in the large generosity of his nature, was always ready to instruct less gifted mortals, who did not always appreciate his unasked services at the value he set upon them. But the errors of the Puritan, like the errors of most well intentioned persons, are but the defects of his qualities, and a vast deal too much has been made of them.

It is a law of nature that those who have had the hardest lives shall become the most rigid in character, and the New-Englanders have always had the fame of having fulfilled this natural law to an undue, even to an unnatural, extent, being harsh to cruelty to all who displeased them, including their own sons and daughters; but in this garret full of papers, mostly written by persons who were Calvinists of Calvinists, Puritans of the straitest sect, I am happy to state that I have found many evidences of kindnesses most tenderly bestowed and gratefully received, and of deeds of a large-minded tolerance and charity, as well as of tender and even demonstrative affection, including a good deal of jocose familiarity between parents and children. On the other hand, I have found record of but very few things that manifest intolerance or hard feelings; and these were all in the earlier years, when the harshness engendered by the persecutions from which the colonists had fled and by the terrors of the wilderness to which they had come had not had time to mellow into patience and forbearance. Neither (except in the papers relating to suits at law which had been conducted by or before one of the ablest lawyers and judges of his time, and with which none of the families or persons connected with those whose lives we picture had anything to do) is there aught to show malice, trickery, or disgrace of any sort. These family records are simple, but, thank God! they are clean. The material hardships of the new land were very great, but most severely felt were the trials of homesickness, the longing for a sight or a token of those who had been left in the homes beyond the sea, and the lack of facilities for the mental culture of their children. The determination to reduce the latter difficulty as soon as might be was evidenced in the early establishment of the two upper-grade schools which were ambitiously termed the colleges of Harvard and Yale, so called not because of what they were or could be at the start, but because of the high standing to which it was confidently hoped they would ultimately attain.

Rudimentary schools were defective in many ways, but the teachers did their best to make zeal atone for the lack of other essentials. The grandchildren of the first immigrants appear to have suffered much more from the want of proper instruction than did the preceding and the next following generation, but never, from first to last, did they cease to set the highest value upon intellectual cultivation or fail of using every means in their power to secure for their children the advantages of a "polite education," a phrase which is repeated hundreds of times in these old letters. Spelling was evidently considered as a matter of the slightest consequence by the first settlers as well as their successors. I have preserved the orthography of the originals in the papers from which I have quoted, in deference to the views of others rather than my own, because it seems to me to convey a wrong impression regarding the degree of cultivation of the writers. English is even now the worst spelled language in the world, and in days not so very long past dictionaries were rare and costly, besides which they differed widely between themselves.

Partly because I have lived so long in the companionship of the old papers, and partly because in my youth I listened with such an intense interest to the family traditions as they fell from the lips of wonderfully gifted narrators, whose words clothed the dead with life, bringing them before the eye and making their voices distinct to the ear, all the persons of whose simple ways of living I have tried to give glimpses seem as familiarly known to me as are the dear relatives through whom so much that concerned their ancestry was transmitted to me.

And why should it not be so? The old letters are still pulsing with the inner life of those who have merely stepped beyond the curtain. Their loves, their fears, their hopes, their aspirations, their faiths, their daily occupations — did not these things form the real men and women? And all these

have heen faithfully preserved in the unaffected
chronicles of fathers and mothers, brothers and
sisters, friends and lovers, who wrote for the limited
circle of those whom they loved and who loved
them; and prove them to be worthy of the love
of those who came after them.

CHAPTER III

A PIONEER PARSON

CHAPTER III.

A PIONEER PASTOR.

Rev. Henry Smith of Wethersfield, Connecticut.

Troubles of a Wilderness Church.

Letter from Samuel Smith of Hadley, Massachusetts, in 1698, describing Early Days in Wethersfield.

The Minister's Will.

I N New England the life of family, church, and town began together. The immigrants mostly came in families. Of bachelors there were a few; but these, by wise forethought, were attached, at least temporarily, to some one of the families very soon after the landing, if not actually during the voyage. As the earliest colonists were almost wholly persons who came here through religious motives, such heads of families as were of the most social note were naturally among the most active in church matters, and therefore in those of the town; for during many years the church was practically the town also, the elders or deacons of the one usually being the selectmen of the other.

The church edifice could not be erected at as early a date as the houses; but in many cases the church had been organized even before the selection of the town site, and the most commodious of the dwellings was used as a meeting-house as soon as it could afford a shelter from the weather. By prescriptive rights the ministers were the lead-

ing citizens in each town. They were often, perhaps generally, men of gentle birth, and usually
graduates of one of the leading universities — most
frequently of Cambridge, that "nursery of Puritan-
ism"; thus they were naturally the social as well
as the spiritual leaders of their people. As eccle-
siastics they seem to have deemed themselves, and
to have been esteemed by their congregations, to
be divine-right priests and Levites, with authority
to declare and enforce the law of the Lord. Yet
it is said that the title of Reverend was not used in
New England until 1670; ministers before that
time being called Mister, Pastor, Teacher, or Elder,
save in a few instances where deceased ministers
were spoken of as Reverend Elders. To their
honor be it spoken that, notwithstanding their
conceded superiority, there were very few of these
ministers who did not bear themselves as servants
under authority and strictly accountable to the
Master whom they loyally served for the just exercise of the power which he had delegated to
them. They ruled their people, but it was with a
father's despotism — as loving and as gentle as it
was strong.

With a few exceptions, the rule of the pastors
was, for more than a century, almost unquestioned,
because it was in the main both wise and unselfish.
In the family life of the colonial pastors we find
the beginnings of all that is best in the history of
our country: the charity that begins at home, but

is not confined to family, church, or township; the warm affections, the sturdy honesty, the firm adherence to what is deemed to be right; the courageous confession when a wrong is recognized, and, as speedily as may be, a contrite atonement made. It has been said of the half-century pastorate of a descendant of the pioneer pastor the faint traces of whose footsteps we are now about to follow,— and the words apply to many others,— that " The town's history from the day of the Pastor's installation might almost be said to be his biography, with a few foot notes of other things. . . . He was a kind of college in himself . . . sending out, like class after class, the influences, the growths and inspirations of his large nature upon the lives of the men and women of his flock."

Trumbull, in his history of Connecticut, having previously designated the chief settlers of Windsor and Hartford, names those of Wethersfield, giving Mr. Henry Smith as among the latter, and adds: " These were the civil and religious Fathers of a Colony that formed its free and happy constitution, they were its legislators and some of the chief pillars of the church and commonwealth, they . . . employed their ability and their estates for the prosperity of the Colony."

Nearly half, if not more than half, of the stanch first settlers of Connecticut had left England after the opening of the eleven years of terror which began with the prorogation of Parliament in 1629.

During these years Archbishop Laud and the Earl of Strafford were held by the loyal-hearted among the people to be responsible for all the sins of their master, and doubtless some of the odium that the advisers received was richly merited; but Laud, at least, although a bigot and a fanatic, was both able and honest, while Charles had all the bigotry and the fanaticism, without the honesty, of him whom he made his tool.

Very heavy fines, the loss of stipends justly due, and imprisonment for too great freedom of speech, were among the minor punishments inflicted upon the clergy and laymen who did not acquiesce in the doctrines inculcated by those in authority. These, and the despair of better days coming in the old England, were the considerations which drove the great body of our Puritan settlers to take the desperate step of emigrating to the New England. Even this was not permitted without much opposition from the officers of the crown. A few persons would meet privately, agree upon one or two men as leaders, and empower them to secure and charter a suitable ship, shipmaster, and crew, and to lay in the necessary stores for the voyage and the subsequent plantation in the wilderness. Those who wished to join the adventure were obliged to sell their landed estates or other property, and also to purchase their personal supplies, mostly at a great disadvantage on account of the necessary secrecy. At all ports of possible departure the government's spies were constantly on the lookout to report tokens of intention to escape. Detection made arrest certain, and imprisonment and confiscation of property almost as certain.

The cost of transportation of human beings, cattle, or freight, in the miserable little vessels of the time, was — considering the difference in the purchasing power of money — enormous. The company which went to Watertown, Massachusetts, brought with them one hundred and eighty servants, whose passage cost the company an average of something over eighty-three dollars each, which was probably equivalent to about two hundred and fifty dollars of our present currency. At this rate the transportation of a large family, with servants and domestic animals, agricultural implements, other essential tools and provisions, not only for the voyage, but for twelve or more months thereafter, and even the most modest outfits of personal and household effects, must have gone far toward exhausting the funds which the adventurers might have derived from the necessarily disadvantageous sales of their property.

It was from Watertown that a great part of the Connecticut Colony came. Some persons were sent ahead, in the summer of 1635, to prepare temporary quarters for the families. The latter, numbering sixty persons in all, men, women, and children, began to move in October of the same year. The journey, which was necessarily on foot,

— there being no paths save the Indian trails, and very few, if any, beasts of burden,— was so long that winter came weeks before the poor creatures were nearly ready for it. "By November 15th," says Trumbull, "the Connecticut River was frozen over and the snow upon it was so deep that a considerable number of the cattle that had been so painfully driven from Massachusetts, could not be got across the River. The sufferings of man and beast were extreme. Their principal provisions and household furniture had been sent around in several small vessels to come up the River. Several of these were wrecked. Great numbers of the cattle perished." The following summer the Rev. Thomas Hooker headed the second company coming from Watertown. It was a pleasanter coming, owing to the more propitious season, and made forever both picturesque and pathetic by the presence of the litter bearing poor, patient Mrs. Hooker, carried as tenderly as might be by the willing hands of her husband's parishioners and fellow-pioneers.

Although the Rev. Henry Smith is historically called the "first settled pastor of the first settled town in Connecticut," it is not probable that he came with either of the first two bands from Watertown, but with a later one. A few log cabins were built in what subsequently became known as the "town of Weathersfield" even before the first settlers reached Windsor. Thus

Wethersfield claims to be the first settled town in the State, and Mr. Smith was its first settled pastor, though he was not installed as such until after Mr. Hooker and Mr. Warham were officiating in Hartford and in Windsor. It is not recorded just when Mr. Smith came to Wethersfield, but he was residing there and received his allotment at the first apportionment of the town lands.

Mr. Smith had reached this country, going first to Watertown, in 1636 or 1637. While the rule in New England pastorates was that the pastor was literally as well as figuratively the head of an obedient flock, which paid him all due deference, and followed his lead as sheep follow the piping of the shepherd, the pastors who successively essayed the charge of the church in Wethersfield were the unfortunate exceptions. In no sense could Mr. Smith have found his new pastorate a bed of roses. Besides the privations and hardships common to all pioneer pastors, there seems to have been a strong and most unusual element of turbulence in the membership of this wilderness church, for two preceding ministers had tried and failed to unite the members of the congregation sufficiently to secure a settlement, and the trouble did not immediately cease upon Mr. Smith's installation. Previous to or about the time of his settlement in Wethersfield the most prominent of the insurgents, under advice of the Rev. John Davenport and others, had removed to Stamford; yet the restless spirits who were left found enough to say against Mr. Smith's ministry during the next few years. There is evidence tending to show that he may have been too liberal in his construction of doctrinal views, and inclined to too great charity in matters of personal conduct, to suit the more rigid among the townsmen. In at least one instance matters went so far that the pastor was brought before the General Court on charges the nature of which is not now apparent; but it is recorded that fines which for that day were very heavy were laid upon certain individuals "for preferring a list of grievances against Mr. Smith and failing to prove in the prosecution thereof." From references to this, which appear in manuscript of about a century after this date, referring to this trial as a thing still remembered, it would seem that Mr. Smith was opposed to severity in church discipline, and also to the importation into the Connecticut Colony of the bribe to hypocrisy which was offered by the law restricting to church-members the right of suffrage in town as well as church matters; and that he also preferred to believe an accused man to be innocent until he was proved guilty, and even then did not believe in proceeding to extremities until after every gentle means had been tried in vain.

One cause of animadversion is said to have been that Mr. Smith had advocated the separation of a wife from a drunken husband who had frightfully abused her and her children. This seems to have been thought by some members of the congregation to indicate great laxity of moral principle on the part of the pastor; but evidently the majority of the people were with him on these and other disputed points, and so were his friends, Mr. Thomas Hooker, the beloved pastor of the church at Hartford, and Mr. Warham of Windsor. Another complaint against Mr. Smith was that he refused to listen to those who brought him reports concerning alleged infractions of church discipline, on the ground that many of these things were matters which lay solely between a man and his Maker. In the end Mr. Smith carried the church with him, and when he died, in 1648, he was sincerely mourned even by those who at one time had " despitefully used " him.

Mr. Smith is said to have been " a scholarly man of gentle birth and breeding, a persuasive preacher and a loyal friend." What his salary may have been does not appear, but the stipends of other pastors of his day rarely exceeded from seventy to seventy-five pounds per annum. Much of this nominal sum was paid " in kind," that is, in farm produce or in peltries, which last were considered as the equivalent of cash, always bringing their fair price in the English markets. One hundred pounds per annum, paid in very much the same way, was an exceptionally good salary more than one hundred and twenty-five years later.

Indians were a very real and imminent danger in the early days of Wethersfield. Their depredations were frequent, and the dread of them was never-ceasing. We do not know whether the first meeting-house of Wethersfield, which was probably the only one erected during Mr. Smith's pastorate, was built of logs or was a frame structure, but we are certain that it was intended to serve not only as a house of worship but for purposes of defense in times of danger, and that, whatever its form or substance, its builders worked in constant fear for their wives and children, with muskets ever at hand and sentinels always on duty.

Another thing we suppose that we know, only because it is true of all other churches of the time, is that it had no chimney. This lack of provision for any means of ameliorating the cold of our winters was not owing, as sometimes believed, to any foolish prejudice or superstition, or, as some seem to think, from mere love of hardships and discomforts on the part of the Puritans, but to the dread of conflagration. Fireless church edifices were then universal, both in Europe and America. Furnaces and even stoves were not, and open fires are dangerous enough even in houses that are inhabited and watched. An open wood fire built in a house that had been closed all the week could scarcely have accomplished more than to thaw the frost from the walls into visible streams of chilly dampness, without greatly raising the temperature by the time that even the prolonged services of the Puritan Sabbath were finished; and the treacherous beds of embers, even after copious waterings, often proved to be unsafe.

Those who could afford such luxuries curtained their square pews to keep currents of air from too great familiarity, cushioned their otherwise comfortless seats, and covered the floors with wolfskins and even sometimes with those of the bear, though the latter were generally too precious for floors.

At as early a date as time and means permitted, small "Sabbath Day Houses" were erected at a certain distance from the sacred edifice. These little buildings were furnished with forms and stools, and here, during the service-time, care-takers were left and fires maintained. From these the coals were taken for the small foot-stoves of which many are still found in old garrets, and which afforded a degree of comfort to the half-frozen church-goers, who at intervals between services were wont to gather in the little houses to warm themselves and exchange neighborly greetings and news. Bitter indeed must sometimes have been their sufferings in cold winter weather, but hardly as great as the same state of things would cause to-day, because no one had yet been rendered unduly tender by furnace- or steam-heated houses. There was not then in the colonies anything that could be termed wealth, but had there been ever so much of it, the treasure of an equably warm temperature could not have been purchased.

Probably the house of the pastor would have been as well built and furnished as those of his neighbors, but in the earliest days that is not saying much for either. Even in the stateliest dwellings of England, though there was sometimes a good deal of luxury and display, there was then very little of what we should esteem to be the necessary comforts of life. In this country the inventories of the seventeenth century reveal the poverty of the land in unmistakable ways. Nothing was too small to escape enumeration, so we know that the poorest farm-laborer of to-day is richer in comforts than the wealthiest of these pioneers.

Few, if any, of the early houses were of more than one story in height. They were built of logs, and rarely contained more than four rooms. An exception to this was the old stone house of Guilford, Connecticut, built in 1639, which was intended to serve as a fortress as well as the minister's residence. Exceptional also were the houses of the Rev. Thomas Hooker and Mr. Whiting of Hartford at the time of their erection. But it was not long before well-constructed, durable, and even handsome dwellings were reared in every colony.

In our own day the lives of pioneers are considered of the hardest; yet now all are within comparatively easy reach of the base of supplies. The

Klondike is not now farther from us than old England was from New England in those early days. Probably but few of the settlers belonged to the wealthy class at home, yet many were numbered among the substantial landowners,— the upper-class yeoman and the lower gentry,— accustomed in their own country to all the comforts then known. Almost all who came between 1628 and 1640 had fled from the persecution under Archbishop Laud which had done so much to bring on the parliamentary wars and the reign of Cromwell, and such refugees had neither thought nor hope of returning. All must have felt their privations keenly, but concerning this we have little recorded complaint or testimony of any sort. The difficulties of transmission were so great that probably few letters were written, and of these but a small number have descended to us.

In the diary of Juliana Smith, 1779–81, there exists a copy of a fragment of a reminiscent letter, written in 1699 by the Rev. Henry Smith's son, Samuel Smith of Hadley, Massachusetts, to his son, Ichabod Smith, residing in Suffield, Connecticut, apparently in reply to some inquiries which the latter had made.

Juliana writes:

" Today my Grandmother Smith gave me to read what is left unburnt of a Letter which was written to my Great-Grandfather by his Father &

has permitted me to copy it. The Letter itself belongs to my Uncle Dan because he is my Grandfather's eldest son. A large part of it was burnt when my Grandfather's house in Suffield took fire, and was barely saved from destruction, with the loss of many things, especially Books & Papers. The Bible in which this Letter was kept was found on the next day still smouldering, with more than half of its leaves burnt away, including a part of the Family Record & this Letter:—

" ' Hadley, Massachusetts Colony,

Jan. ye Firste, $16\frac{28}{99}$

" ' My Dear & Dutiful Son: . . . I was of so tender an Age at the death of my beloved Father that I am possessed of but little of the Information for which you seek. My Revered Father was an ordained Minister of ye Gospelle, educate at Cambridge in England & came to yis Land by reason of ye Great Persecution by which ye infamous Archibishop Laud and ye Black Tom Tyrante, (as Mr. Russell was always wont to call ye Earl of Strafforde,) did cause ye reign of his Majestie Charles ye First to loose favour in ye sight of ye people of England. My Father & Mother came over in $16\frac{36}{37}$, firste to Watertown which is neare Boston, & after a yeare or two to Weathersfield on ye great River, where he became ye firste settled Pastor.

" ' Concerning of ye earlie days I can remember

but little save Hardship. My Parents had broughte bothe Men Servants & Maid Servants from England, but ye Maids tarried not but till they got Married, ye wch was shortly, for there was great scarcity of Women in ye Colonies. Ye men did abide better. Onne of em had married onne of my Mother's Maids & they did come with us to Weathersfield to our grate Comforte for some Yeares, untill they had manny littel onnes of theire Owne. I do well remember ye Face & Figure of my Honoured Father. He was 5 foote, 10 inches talle, & spare of builde, tho not leane. He was as Active as ye Red Skin Men & sinewy. His delighte was in sportes of strengthe & withe his owne Hands he did helpe to rear bothe our owne House & ye Firste Meetinge House of Weathersfield, wherein he preacht yeares too fewe. He was well Featured & Fresh favoured with faire Skin & longe curling Hair (as neare all of us have had) with a merrie eye & swete smilinge Mouthe, tho he coulde frowne sternlie eno' when need was.

" ' Ye firste Meetinge House was solid mayde to withstande ye wicked onsaults of ye Red Skins. Its Foundations was laide in ye feare of ye Lord, but its Walls was truly laide in ye feare of ye Indians, for many & grate was ye Terrors of em. I do mind me y't alle ye able-bodied Men did work thereat, & ye olde & feeble did watch in turns to espie if any Salvages was in hidinge neare

4

& every Man keept his Musket nighe to his
hande.   I do not myself remember any of ye
Attacks mayde by large bodeys of Indians whilst
we did remayne in Weathersfield, but did ofttimes
hear of em.   Several Families wch did live back
a ways from ye River was either Murderdt or
Captivated in my Boyhood & we all did live in
constant feare of ye like.   My Father ever de-
clardt there would not be so much to feare iff ye
Red Skins was treated with suche mixture of Justice & Authority as they cld understand, but iff he
was living now he must see that wee can do
naught but *fight* em & that right heavily.

"'After ye Red Skins ye grate Terror of our
lives at Weathersfield & for many yeares after we
had moved to Hadley to live, was ye Wolves.
Catamounts was bad eno' & so was ye Beares, but
it was ye Wolves yt was ye worst.   The noyes of
theyre howlings was eno' to curdle ye bloode of
ye stoutest & I have never seen ye Man yt did
not shiver at ye Sounde of a Packe of em.   What
wth ye way we hated em & ye goode money yt
was offered for theyre Heads we do not heare em
now so much, but when I do I feel again ye
younge hatred rising in my Bloode, & it is not a
Sin because God mayde em to be hated.   My
Mother & Sister did each of em kill more yan one
of ye gray Howlers & once my oldest Sister shot
a Beare yt came too neare ye House.   He was a
goode Fatte onne & keept us all in meate for a

good while. I guess one of her Daughters has got ye skinne.

"'As most of ye Weathersfield Settlers did come afoot throu ye Wilderness & brought with em such Things only as they did most neede at ye firste, ye other Things was sent round from Boston in Vessels to come up ye River to us. Some of ye Shippes did come safe to Weathersfield, but many was lost in a grate storm. Amongst em was onne wch held alle our Beste Things. A good many Yeares later, long after my Father had died of ye grate Fever & my Mother had married Mr. Russell & moved to Hadley, it was found yt some of our Things had been saved & keept in ye Fort wch is by ye River's Mouthe, & they was brought to us. Most of em was spoilt with Sea Water & Mould, especially ye Bookes [Foot-note by Juliana: "My Father hath one of these books — The vision of Piers Plowman. It is so ruinated with damp and mould yt no one can read ye whole of it."] & ye Plate. Of this there was no grate store, only ye Tankard, wch I have, and some Spoones, divided amongst my Sisters wch was alle so black it was long before any could come to its owne colour agen, & Mr. Russell did opine yt had it not been so it might not have founde us agen, but he was sometimes a littel shorte of ye Charity wch thinketh no Evil, at ye least I was wont to think so when his Hand was too heavy on my Shoulders & I remembered ye sweetnesse & ye Charity of my firste Father, but on ye whole said he was a Goode Man & did well by my Mother & her children, & no doubt we did often try his wit & temper, but it was in his house yt ' —

"Here," writes the copyist, "there is a break " — probably where the sheets of the original had been burned.

The silver tankard mentioned in the foregoing letter of Samuel Smith of Hadley is in all probability the one now belonging to my brother, Gilbert Livingston Smith of Sharon, Connecticut, though the earliest positive record which we have concerning it is in a bill of sale, including various things to the amount of nearly £700, made to the Rev. Cotton Mather Smith by his brother, Simeon Smith, M.D., when the latter was leaving Sharon to take up his residence in Vermont in 1787. It is there described as "One ancient Silver Tankard marked with our coat of arms & S. S., bought by me from Brother Dan." The tankard now has on the side opposite the handle a spout, which was put on about 1820 that it might be used as a water-pitcher. Family tradition has always held that this tankard was brought from England in 1636 by the Rev. Henry Smith, and referred to in the letter just quoted.

Poor and incomplete are these glimpses of a New England pastorate, but they bring before us some of the privations suffered, and the courage which so bravely met them because it was grounded on an unbounded faith in an omnipotent Father, and was cheered by family affection. Of both of these the last will and testament of the Rev. Henry Smith gives beautiful testimony. It is not couched in legal phraseology, but was apparently written by himself, and hence is more than usually expressive of the testator's character. He had not waited until the shadow of death had fallen upon him before making his slender worldly preparations for " departing hence to be no more," but, " Being in health of body and soundness of mind," and " wishing to leave no occasion of trouble for my children," the will was made several months before his decease. There was not much to be disposed of, only a trifle over £370, but that little is so graciously bestowed that one feels as fully persuaded of the testator's own loving heart as he was persuaded of God's " unchangeable love and good will both in life and death . . . according to His covenant, viz: — I am thy God and of thy Seede after thee."

After this profession of faith, which evidently comes from a simple and earnest heart, the will proceeds :

" Then for my ovtward estate, wch, because it is but littel, & I haue well proued the difficvlties of this covntry, how hard a thing it will bee for a

woman to manage the affairs of so great a family
as the Father of Mercyes hath blessed mee withall,
& haue allso experience of the prvdence & faith-
fvlness of my deare Wife, who shall, in parting
withe mee, part allso withe a great part of her liue-
lihood; I do therefore beqveath & giue to her, the
fvll power & disposal of alle that estate wch God
hath gieuen mee, in howses, lands, cattells & goods
whatsoeuer, within dores and withovt; only pro-
uiding that in case shee marry again, or otherwise
shee bee able comfortably to spare it from her own
necessary maintenance, that shee giue vnto my
Sonne Samvell that part of my hovse lott that was
intended for my Sonne Peregrine lyinge next to
the bvrying place, & the land I haue beyon the
great Riuer eastward; & allso, to him & my second Sonne, Noah, fiue acres apeece of meadow
with vplands proportionable therevnto, & to the
reste of my children vnmarried, 20 pounds apeece,
at the age of one & twenty yeares, or at the time
of her death, wch shall come the sooner. & for
my two Davghters that bee married, my desire is
that they haue 20 Shillings apeece and euery onne
of their children fiue Shillings apeece, either in
bookes or such other things as my Wife shall best
please to part withall."

Of the £370 nearly one half was in houses and
lands, £50 were in live stock, which did not
include any domestic fowls, the latter being still

scarce in the colonies. Bees, number of hives not stated, were valued at £8, which seemingly disproportionately large valuation was probably due to the scarcity of the cultivated variety. Probably Mr. Smith was, as all the New England pastors of his time were obliged to be, a farmer as well as a preacher, but he could not have been enthusiastically devoted to agriculture, for his "husbandry tools" were only valued at £3 10s., while his "armes & ammunition" were reckoned at £4.

"Bookes" are mentioned, but their value not estimated, probably because at the time of his death, during a prevailing "grate fever," proper appraisers may not have been on hand. Ministers were usually appointed to appraise books. Out of thirty-seven inventories which were recorded during the first ten years of the Connecticut Colony, in only nine, including that of Mr. Smith, do we find mention of books. The total value of these in six of the nine is estimated at £39 13s. Mr. Hooker's books were estimated at £300, a considerable item in an estate amounting to only about £1136. I say "only" when viewing this subject from present conditions; under those of 1648 in the colonies, Mr. Hooker was a wealthy man. His friend and parishioner, Mr. William Whiting, the plutocrat of the Connecticut Colony, left an estate of £2854, including debts due to him which are classed as "doubtful," and "adventures wch are harserdous" to the amount of £429. His "books & apparell" united are appraised at £25.

What would seem to be a disproportionately costly item in Mr. Smith's house furnishings was that of beds. Bedsteads are not named, perhaps because there were none, for there were comparatively few in the country, save the sleeping-bunks built in with the houses, until fifteen or twenty years later than this. "Three feather beds with all things belonging to them" are valued at £40, which would seem to show that the "all things" were of extra quality, or that the other usual furnishings of the bedrooms, and perhaps also that of the parlor or living-room, as well as the beds themselves, were included in that valuation.

Probably it was for the accommodation of fire that the parlor was usually the guest bedroom, and we find that the entire parlor furniture of the wealthy Mr. Whiting, including "bed-stead, bed, stools, a clock [perhaps the only one in the colony], a safe [probably an iron or steel chest like those preserved in some European museums], a cradle, cob irons," etc., is altogether valued at only £17 3s.

Mr. Smith's tables, chairs, stools, cushions, and "other things belonging" are altogether valued at £3 15s., while "cob irons, trammels & other fire irons" were valued at £2 8s., and "brasse, iron potts, pewter & such like" were appraised at £15. The two classes of goods last mentioned, which at that date must have been imported, would naturally cost more than the tables and stools, which, however roughly, could be made here. Probably there were not more than two or three chairs, and these would have been brought from England. Table and other linen and a "carpett" (that is, a table-cover) were valued at £14 10*s*.

After 1650 the variety and value of the personal property mentioned in the inventories rapidly increased, while the number of inventories does not keep pace with the number of wills probated or of estates administered upon, the wealthier and more intelligent members of the community preferring probably to keep such information within the privacy of the family circle, not having prevision of how eagerly all such information would be welcomed by that posterity for which they prayed and toiled and hoped, dimly feeling all the while that this great new land had been set apart for great uses in the days which were to follow their own.

A glimpse of the relation which then existed between a Puritan pastor and his flock may be gained from the following, which is the closing paragraph of Mr. Smith's will:

"And I desire the Church whose seruant I now am, to take the care and ouersight of my family that they may be brovght vp in the trve feare of God, and to see that this my Will be faithfvlly prformed. In witnesse whereof I haue svbscribed my name the 8th day of May, 1648."

CHAPTER IV

A PIONEER HOME IN CONNECTICUT

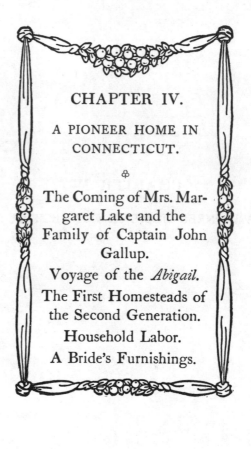

CHAPTER IV.

A PIONEER HOME IN CONNECTICUT.

✤

The Coming of Mrs. Margaret Lake and the Family of Captain John Gallup.
Voyage of the *Abigail*.
The First Homesteads of the Second Generation.
Household Labor.
A Bride's Furnishings.

AMONG the many slow-sailing craft of petty tonnage which followed in the wake of the *Mayflower*, there were not a few which brought men and women of high future importance to the infant colonies of New England; but probably few had a more notable passenger list than that of the little ship *Abigail*, which, after a ten weeks' voyage, reached Boston in November, 1635. Of its two hundred and twenty passengers some bore names which were already noted in old England, and the names of others were afterward to become distinguished in the New. Among the latter was the second John Winthrop, the founder of Ipswich, Massachusetts, and afterward the honored governor of Connecticut Colony for many successive terms. With him came his second wife, then newly wed, and her elder sister, Mrs. Margaret Lake, with her two young daughters. It is with Mrs. Lake, rather than with any of the more distinguished members of this notable ship's company, that our present chapter is concerned.

Not until twelve years after the arrival of the

Abigail do we again hear of Mrs. Lake. This time it is as the first white woman to set foot in what is now New London County, where — and a very unusual thing it was at that time — she is named as one of the original grantees, sharing in all the grants and divisions of land. Mrs. Lake probably never took up her residence in New London, appearing to have shared the home of her sister, Mrs. Winthrop, until the latter's husband became the governor of Connecticut Colony, after which period Mrs. Lake continued to reside in Ipswich, perhaps in the house which had belonged to the Winthrops. It was on the portion of land which had been assigned to Mrs. Lake in New London County that her daughter Hannah, when, in 1643, she had become the wife of the second Captain John Gallup, lived for the first few years of her wedded life.

Although the conditions of life were necessarily of the hardest all through the early days in all the colonies, and there is no doubt that they were hardest of all in sterile New England, it must not be imagined that there were no degrees in the styles of living. In spite of the leveling effect of common sentiments, circumstances, privations, and dangers, and of the fact that men of gentle birth and cultivated minds were forced by the first law of nature to become measurably skilled in all sorts of handicraft, class distinctions were for several generations as rigorously maintained in the

New England as in the Old. It was said by
Daniel Neal, writing in 1720: "In their Dress,
Tables and Conversation, they [the colonists]
affect to be as English as possible. . . . The only
difference between an Old and a New English
Man is in his Religion." Hence it is plain that,
at least after the first two or three years in any
given settlement, to describe the home of a family
belonging to one social class is by no means to
describe that of a family belonging to another
class at the same, much less at another, period.

The wills of the respective ancestors of John
and of Hannah Lake Gallup prove them to have
been men of considerable substance and local importance in old England. In the New World
their family alliances were equally respectable, so
it may be supposed that their dwelling and home
belongings were fairly representative of those of
the best of the pioneer families of their time.

But before the nest-building must have come
the mating, with all its preliminaries, as sweet
here in the wilderness as if the actors in the little
love-drama had been walking beneath the haw-
thorn hedges on one of their ancestral manors
across the sea. Between the dust-dry lines of the
dim old records we imagine that we catch a
glimpse of what may have been a very charming
and beautiful romance; for John Gallup and
Hannah Lake, as boy and girl, probably about
fourteen and twelve years of age, were fellow-pas-

sengers on the ship *Abigail* during the long cross-
ing of the stormy Atlantic. When, as in this
case, more than two hundred passengers were
packed closely together for ten or more tedious
and sometimes fearful weeks, there is no doubt
that the foundations were laid for many long-
enduring friendships, and sometimes, alas! for
equally durable dislikes; and if these, why may
not love also have been born in these confined
and tempestuous quarters? At least, it is a pleasant thought, with some warrant of tradition and
probability, that the manly boy, tall, handsome,
and bold as he must have been, if in this case the
boy was the father of the man, and the bright-
faced girl who became a brave, high-spirited, and
loving matron, may have begun their mutual lifelong trust and love upon this wave-tossed little
vessel, smaller than many a fishing-schooner of
to-day. There must certainly have been many
opportunities to make their respective faults and
virtues known to each other.

The conditions of such a voyage are vividly
painted in the elder Governor Winthrop's journal
of his own voyage five years preceding that of the
Abigail. He makes no complaints, but it is easy
to see that the noble spirit of the adventurer for
conscience' sake had much to triumph over. On
the four vessels of which the bark which bore him
was one, he records that there were three deaths
and three births during the voyage. Surely those

were brave women who accompanied their husbands, venturing so much at such a time! One
advantage that the elder Winthrop's company had,
and which probably they of the younger did not
have, has a picnicky sound that is droll enough to
modern ears.

When "off the banks of New Foundland the
Arabella stopped to fish,"* and "all the passengers
who were so minded" seem to have enjoyed the
sport of replenishing their scanty larder. A little
later we find that they were picking strawberries
on Cape Ann.

The *Abigail's* weary voyage was not ended until
in November, much too late for any such diversions. It is at least to be hoped that her passengers did not, like those of a ship which immediately
followed the *Arabella*, "arrive nearly starved,"
but it is certain that they had on board a most
unwelcome companion in the smallpox. At that
time even inoculation had not become known, and
we can now but faintly imagine the well-justified
terrors of those exposed to the disease.

Though the young couple were not married
until eight years after their arrival in this country,
it is probable that their earliest dwelling was built
of logs, as were most of the houses of this date and
vicinity. If so, it was soon superseded by the
permanent homestead, which was not taken down
until the latter part of the eighteenth century. I
have talked about this house with a man who had

heard it described by his mother, the daughter of a farm-laborer who had lived in it until her marriage at the age of eighteen years. Soon after that time it ceased to be used as a dwelling, and before this it had long been occupied only as a tenement-house for farm-laborers, a finer residence having been erected for their own homestead by the descendants of the builders of the first. The second permanent home of the Gallups was fine for its days and must have been intended to fill, in a degree, the place of one of the old manor-houses, of which the builders of the first had probably transmitted vivid memory-pictures; but the dwelling which immediately succeeded the log house was erected with a view to meeting the needs of the new country.

That so few of the houses of the early settlers were built of the excellent stone which is over-abundant in New England was not due to the groundless prejudice against that material which arose among their great-grandchildren, but to the fact that haste — such haste as was possible in those slow days — was of the utmost consequence. No man wished to spend the best years of his life in a cabin of logs and clay while waiting for a stone house to grow, as ordinarily it must under the tedious methods of the period, layer by layer, the lower tiers almost having time to gather moss before the roof-beams could be raised.

The larger part of the best of the early houses

of New England were probably much like this first permanent homestead of the Gallups. Both the external walls and those of the partitions were of heavy timbers, roughly squared by the ax, chinked with moss, and lined with hewn planks two inches in thickness. In later days coats of plaster were put on over the planks, but during the first years the walls were made warm as well as picturesque by hangings of bear, deer, otter, wild-cat, and fox skins, whenever these could be spared from more pressing uses. The exterior walls were about two feet in thickness, which tells of the size of the forest trees which had been cut down to make them. The high-placed and deep-seated windows were scant in number, heavily barred and narrow. (The Pequots and Narragansetts were near, numerous, and crafty.) It is doubtful if the first of the windows were glazed. Even in old England it was only the wealthy who at this time could afford the luxury of glass. Oiled paper was the usual substitute. To exclude the cold were heavy and close wooden shutters both outside and inside. During the coldest weather it must have been necessary to depend for light, even in the daytime, upon open fires, pine-knots, and candles, for at least the first decade or two in each new settlement.

In the center of the house rose the great stone chimney, with wide-throated fireplaces opening into three large rooms on the first story, and into four upon the second story. The unplastered and paintless ceilings were low, but higher than was usual, for John Gallup is said to have stood six feet four inches in his gray knit hose, and had to bow his stately head to enter any doorway save his own. The second story on the two longer sides projected considerably beyond the lower. In view of the constant danger from Indians, it is probable that this house was intended to be used as a fortress in case of necessity, and this projection may have been made for the sake of affording a coign of vantage to its inmates if attacked by savages, although, as this method of construction was a common one in nearly all parts of Europe at the time, this is not a necessary supposition. The third story was but a big garret with windows in each end. Beneath all were deep cellars for the storage of winter supplies, and for the manufacture and ripening of home-brewed beer, made after recipes brought from the mother-country. At first cider had no place in those cellars, but after the orchards had grown, there was found room for the barrels of hard cider which were made from them, and which finally quite displaced the heavier and perhaps more wholesome, certainly less stimulating, beer. In the cellars were also kept, even from the first, the casks of metheglin, made from the plentiful honey of the wild bee, which in the autumn filled the place with the sound of its working like the swarming of armies of bees — a sound which was said to be reproduced in the befuddled heads of those who were not extremely moderate in their draughts of this too potent liquor.

In the broad and high-peaked garret were set the heavy looms at which, during all the long summer days, either men or women, as the case might be, were diligently weaving the coarse stuff which must serve young and old, master and man, mistress and maid, for all the rougher occasions of pioneer life.

Very different are the social standards of differing times. In early New England, and in all the colonies, for that matter, it was only a specially wealthy family which could afford to own a loom, at least until they could be made here. Weaving was heavy work, and was mostly done by weavers who went from house to house, or by the poorer neighbors, who were paid in cloth or in other needed supplies. It seems certain that, during the first two or three decades at least, much of the spinning must have been done with the distaff, for comparatively few wheels are mentioned in the inventories of those years. Whether with distaff or wheel, spinning was winter's lighter task, and performed by both mistress and maids; but, as with the weaving, it was only the well-to-do who had the materials. It was many years before sufficient wool or flax could be grown in this country to make them plentiful.

Long before cloth-weaving factories were established here, yet not until the early part of the
eighteenth century, a few fulling-mills were set
up; at these the woolen cloths were dyed, fulled,
sheared, and pressed. A web of cloth which had
passed through the fuller's processes was an object
of envy to those — and they were in the majority
— who could not afford to pay for his services.

The making of the plainest linens was probably
all done at home, either with or without the aid of
the itinerant weaver, whose services were sometimes bespoken months in advance, so greatly was
he in demand. Even after his labors were done
the fabric was not ready for use. In my dear
mother's girlhood flax-spinning was still considered as an essential accomplishment for young
ladies, at least among the descendants of the
Huguenots. I have heard her say that to bring
the fine linen for shirts to the required degree of
snowiness no less than thirty and sometimes even
forty bleachings were necessary. The first few
bleachings were of the thread. The colonists were
never sparing of their labor, yet it is probable that
they were not so dainty as to the shade of whiteness in the overfilled days of the seventeenth century. With their best diligence, the time required
from the sowing of the flax to the end of the last
bleaching could never be less than sixteen months.

Farm-laborers had come over in numbers, and
there was a fair proportion of mechanics, but of

maid-servants there was oftentimes a great lack. Though many a family, among the richer colonists, had brought several, the maid-servants were always fewer in number than the men-servants, and when they married, as most of them did very soon, there was no way of supplying their places. At the date when this old house was new there were few negroes in New England, and the half-tamed squaws who were sometimes employed made very poor substitutes for trained house-workers. As the Winthrops were sometimes most unhappily forced to make use of this very unsatisfactory form of household service, it is probable that Mrs. Lake and her daughters were also compelled to accept of it in default of better.

Scanty enough, according to our standard, were then the plenishings of the wealthy houses of old England, and really pathetic was the scarcity here of what were even then esteemed to be essential comforts in the older land.

Not until well into the second half of the seventeenth century was furniture of any but the roughest sorts made in New England, and it is obviously impossible that much should have been imported in the tiny vessels then dignified by the name of ships. Their space was too important to be filled with furniture, their petty holds being always crowded with the literally indispensable articles, such as provisions, arms, ammunition, tools, seeds, and clothes, while their scanty deck-space was made still scantier by the presence of the live stock of which the colonists were in such pressing need.

In 1645 Mrs. Lake sent to a correspondent in England a list of things which she desired for the furnishing of the new house of her daughter, Mrs. Gallup.   She asked for:

"A peare of brasse Andirons,
A brasse Kittell,
2 grate Chestes well made,
2 armed Cheares with fine rushe bottums,
A carven Caisse for Bottels wch my Cuzzen
    Cooke has of mine,
A Warmeing Pann,
A big iron Pott,
6 Pewter Plates,
2 Pewter Platters,
3 Pewter Porringeres,
A small stew Pann of Copper,
A peare of Brasse and a peare of Silver Candle-
    sticks (of goode Plate.)
A Drippe Panne,
A Bedsteede of carven Oake, (ye one in wch I
    sleept in my Father's house, wth ye Val-
    lances and Curtayns and Tapestry Cover-
    lid belongynge, & ye wch my Sister Bread-
    cale [?] hath in charge for Mee.)
3 Duzzen Nappekins of fine linen damasque &
    2 Tabel cloathes of ye same.   Alsoe 8

fine Holland Pillowe Beeres & 4 ditto
Sheetes,

A skellet,

A pestel & Mortar,

A few Needels of differnt sizes,

A Carpet [that is, a table-cover; the name was
then universally thus applied], of goodley
stuffe and colour, aboute 2 Ell longe.

6 Tabel Knifes of ye beste Steal wth such han-
dels as may bee.

Alsoe, 3 large & 3 smal Silvern Spoones, & 6
of horne."

And this is all. Yet for the time and place it
must have been considered a fine outfit, perhaps
too much so for the wife of the frontier farmer,
skipper, and fighter. At the same period in old
England, in the wills of wealthy titled families,
bedding, utensils of copper, and dishes of pewter
were constantly named as articles of considerable
value. The elder Governor Winthrop was known
as one of the wealthiest of the early colonists, yet
the inventory of his possessions, made in 1649,
does not present a proportionately finer showing.
Even a century later than this date a complete
outfit of pewter plates, dishes, and spoons made a
lordly wedding present, given by a grandson of
Major-General Humphrey Atherton to his daughter — a gift which, according to traditions, excited
some heartburnings among relatives who had not

been so favored. In the absence of pewter, wooden bowls, trenchers, and noggins were considered rather fine, while the carefully dried gourds and the deep, saucer-like shells of the immense quahogs, which were then so abundant, but have now left only degenerate descendants along the New England coasts, served an ever-useful purpose when the supply of better things was short. It is said that small clam-shells, set in split sticks for handles, were used as teaspoons until the early part of this century. The large and thin shells of a kind of scallop, which is still plentiful along the shores of Maine and Massachusetts, are sometimes used even now as skimmers — a curious survival of an old custom so long after the need for it has passed by !

Many years after the old Gallup house had been torn down, the dining-table which had served the family for at least one generation was preserved in an out-house, where my informant had seen it in his youth. It was simply what once had been the cover of a large packing-box, of smooth oak boards, supported by carefully squared legs. The box might have been used to bring the bedding and other things from Europe, for on the under side of the table's top still remained the inscription : " For Mrs. Margarette Lake, Ippsitch."

Chairs, when found at all in the houses of the earliest colonists, were reserved for the heads of families and their most honored guests, or for the infirm. When one remembers what uncomfortable things the most of those chairs were, one must profoundly pity the infirm! One may be permitted to hope that the comfortable " barrel chair," still sometimes found in the country houses, was the happy invention of this time, by some benefactor of the ill and aged. Coopers were plentier than cabinet-makers in those days, and the barrel chair has an extremely primitive look. Even in England, until after the Restoration, backless benches and stools formed the usual seats, and we must suppose that they did so for many years later than that.

Closets or pantries were not often built in the houses which first succeeded the log cabins of the settlers, chests which might also be utilized as seats, and a small room with shelves not always overnicely smoothed, answering for the safe-keeping of most articles not in daily use. A cupboard was a possession indicating a good degree of prosperity, while a " court cup-board," or a sideboard, was a mark of positive affluence, even at a much later date than this.

Scanty as was the wedding house-plenishing of Hannah Gallup, she was reasonably well provided with fine clothes. Indeed, all of the better class among the colonists seem to have had disproportionately liberal supplies of " mantels " and " pettycotes " of velvet or brocade, with other " garments to consort therewith "; but this was not due so much to vanity as to thrift, the best being literally the cheapest in the days when the finer fabrics were so honestly made as to wear for decades, and the cost of carriage was the same for a coat of frieze as for one of velvet.

Of silverware there was some, but not frequent, mention in wills and inventories, and to jewelry still less reference is made, unless mourning-rings may be thus classed. Mrs. Lake bequeathed to one of her daughters an " enamailed " and to the other a " gould " ring. An item of curious interest in this will is the following:

" To my Daughter, Martha Harris, I give my tapestry coverlid and all my other apparell, which are not disposed of to others pticulerly, and I give unto her my mantel, and after her decease to all her children *as their need is*." (The italics are mine.)

Tradition runs that this " mantel " was of Russian sable, even then as costly as it was rare, and that it had been brought from the far East, perhaps China. Such a bequest brings many things to mind: long, tedious sledgings, when stalwart men took the place of horses or oxen and drew their wives or sisters through the windings of wintry forests, where the only track was an Indian trail, and where every step was shadowed by the ever-present dread of the approach of the stealthy foe. Or we see visions of night campings, made fearful by the howlings of the wolves; and, day or night, always the same benumbing cold. Often must the grandmother's fur " mantel " (worn, we may be sure, until the last hair was gone) have proved a veritable life-preserver in those bitter years.

In addition to the above-mentioned " mantel," Mrs. Lake seems to have left a wardrobe of considerable extent and richness, besides a goodly list of linens and other household treasures, with several carved chests to contain them; but no books are mentioned, save a " grate Byble " and " another Bible."

Of such homely comforts as could be made from the materials at hand the industrious and ingenious colonist might possess a rude abundance. Le Grand Monarque of the most luxurious country then existing might have a fine silken instead of a coarse linen slip for his bed, but it would be filled with feathers no better than those plucked from the wild water-fowl of the New England coast; while heavily lined curtains of coarse homespun wool or linen shut out the bitter winds as effectually as the bravest damask from the looms of Flanders. The absence of many things which we now deem to be essential was not felt as a privation, because the things were unknown, not only in this wilderness, but in the old country.

Some one writing of the Lady Arbella Johnson has said that " she came from a paradise of plenty and pleasure into a wilderness of wants." This expression is especially correct as regards its last clause. "A wilderness of wants" this certainly must have seemed, not only to the sister of the Earl of Lincoln, but also to the hardiest of the colonists; and these wants were actual, not imaginary, as evidenced by the frightful death-rates of the early years. But even the tapestried halls the delicate Lady Arbella had left would seem comfortless enough to the daughter of any small farmer of modern New England, however much she might admire its splendor, could she now suddenly find herself placed in the Lady Arbella's fine abode of "pleasure and plenty" as the latter had left it in 1630.

Floor-coverings were then a rarity even in palaces, and the sand and rushes which polished the boards or silenced the tread were as plentiful here as elsewhere. Porcelain was a luxury in any land; even delft was uncommon; and pewter was considered too fine for the daily use of any save the rich. Wooden dishes served on ordinary occasions in old England as in the New, save among the wealthiest. The sense of real privation was felt in things much closer to the needs of the primitive man.

Great, very great, must have been the suffering from the cold and from the lack of suitable food. If the colonists sometimes took undue quantities of beer and the stronger liquors, not only the traditions of the older land but the hard conditions of the new must be remembered in extenuation. They needed something besides cold water. Hot water had not been dreamed of as a beverage, and the milder stimulants of our day had not been introduced. The earliest mention of chocolate in Connecticut is said to have been in 1679. Five years later coffee is first named, and tea not until 1695.

For many years raised bread was hardly known, and this for several very good reasons. It was a difficult matter to preserve the leaven from one baking until the next. Either it would sour from too great heat, or it would lose its vitality from the severe cold weather. To bake bread in an iron pot over the fire or under the same utensil inverted before the blaze, was an undertaking very doubtful in its results; yet there was no other way, for the brick or stone ovens of a later date did not exist during the first decade, and, except in a few instances, probably not for a score of years longer. Until a sufficiency of bread-stuffs could be raised here, which was not for several years, both wheat flour and oatmeal were imported in considerable quantities; but the first was costly even in England, and as both often arrived here in an exceedingly damaged condition, the roughly pounded or ground meal of Indian corn was for months at a time the staff of life — a staff which, for persons of weak powers of digestion, has often proved an insufficient support.

For grinding this the only mills were of the simple Indian construction — a large stone hollowed by natural or by artificial means, and another stone into which a wooden handle had been fitted. The latter was sometimes tied to a young sapling growing near, which, by its rebound, saved the grinder the labor of lifting the pestle. In my childhood near the ruins of an ancient house stood a very large birch-tree; beneath it was a hollow stone, and still lingering amid the upper branches, which had grown in such a way as to hold and support it, could be seen one of these ancient pestles.

After the first few seasons summer vegetables were as fine and as plentiful as in old England, but it was impossible to preserve for winter use any that could not survive deep burial in trenches out of doors or in the cellars, overlaid with piles of earth mixed with dead leaves, so bitter was the winter frost and so inadequate the means of excluding it.

Poultry was more easily brought than larger live stock, and multiplied more rapidly, but it was a good many years after the landing at Plymouth before cows and sheep became plenty. Even as late as 1672, when Mrs. Lake made her will, a "cow and heifer" were evidently esteemed to be bequests of more than ordinary value; indeed, the same was then true in old England, where a man whose estate went by entail to his eldest son, and who bequeathed £1000 each to four younger sons,

seems to have thought each of his daughters well
portioned with £200, a cow, a heifer, ten sheep,
and a feather-bed. Trumbull, in his history of
Connecticut, gives the value of a good milch cow,
at about 1640, as £30. At the same date carpenters and other mechanics were receiving from
fourteen to eighteen pence per day. The work of
a "paire of Oxen with tacklin" was held to be
worth two shillings and fivepence for "six howers"
in winter and "eight howers" the rest of the year,
these hours making the full day's work for cattle,
except in heavy upland plowing, when "six
howers" was considered enough. A man's working hours were reckoned from sun to sun in summer, and from six to six o'clock in winter; but
cattle were much more precious than men. The
latter usually managed to survive the long and
arduous sea voyage, but of the cattle which formed
the deck-load of nearly all incoming ships in
summer, not more than twenty-five per cent. were
expected to survive, even under exceptionally favorable conditions.

Some of the first of the colonists sent by nearly
every returning ship for seeds and young fruit-
trees, but comparatively few of the latter survived
the long voyage, and of course those that did so
required some years to come to maturity. This
led to the making large use of the delicious wild
berries in their seasons, but the best of these, as
the raspberries and the strawberries,— which have

6

sadly degenerated in size since Winthrop tanta-
lized his home correspondents by describing individual berries as "two inches in length,"—do not
take kindly to being dried, refusing to retain their
flavor under such treatment, and no other method
of preservation was then practicable.

Of such fruits as did endure the process great
quantities were gathered and dried, a labor which
added not a little to the toils of the women of the
families during the summer. Under these conditions, it is not wonderful that the useful, long-suffer-
ing pumpkin came into such universal favor.
Preserving fruits by the only effectual method
then known, except drying,—the boiling with the
solid pound of fruit for pound of sugar,—was un-
wholesome, very costly, and but little attempted.
Game and fish were abundant and delicious. Salt
meats were a staple import, and swine soon became
plenty; but horned cattle, sheep, and even domestic
fowls were for a long time too valuable to be eaten.

For years there seems to have been little attempt
at butter-making; most of that which was used
here was imported from England, and often did
not keep well, in spite of being frequently made
unpalatable by the quantity of salt used to preserve it. On the occasion of the wedding of her
daughter Hannah, Mrs. Lake writes that she had
"made some very goode buttere although it
seemed almost Wicket to soe yuse ye milk yt is
so sore needet for ye sick & ye littell ownes."

Sheep were spared for their wool and poultry for their eggs; when the chickens were sacrificed their feathers were carefully preserved, for in those days of scarcity a bed of hen feathers would not be despised, though those of the wild geese and ducks would certainly be more highly prized.

In later times there was no lack of material to keep the hands of matrons and maids busily spinning, but at first there was neither flax nor wool to spin. Woolen yarns were among the articles sent for to England; but threads from worn-out woolen garments long supplied much of the material for the stockings and mittens for working wear.

In these pioneer days the energies of the colonists were devoted to getting together the raw materials for a civilized existence. In 1640 the "Generall Court" of Connecticut Colony issued the following recommendation:

"Whereas as yt is observed yt experience has made appear that much ground within these libertyes may be well improved both in Hempe & Flaxe & yt we myght in time have a supply of lynnen cloath amongst o'selves and for the more speedy procuring of Hempe Seede It is Ordered yt every family within these plantations shall pr'cure and plante this pr'sent yeare at lest onne spoonfull of English hempe seed in fruitful soyle at lest a foot distant betwixt each seed, and the same so planted shall be pr'served and kept in husbandly manner for supply of seed another yeare."

The following year the same ordinance was repeated; after that it may be supposed that enough seed had been secured for future planting.

At what an humble distance must we now admire the indomitable and uncomplaining courage with which these colonists bore their material as well as their more than material privations. To one grievous privation I have seen no reference made as such. Perhaps it bore so heavily upon loving hearts that they feared to give expression to their feelings, and so lift the flood-gates of their suppressed sorrows.

There is preserved a letter written by Mrs. Lake when she had been living in this country twenty-eight years. Her beloved brother-in-law, Winthrop, had gone to England in the interests of the colonists, and Mrs. Lake thus writes to him:

"I would desire you to inquire whether my sister Breadcale bee livinge, you may hear of her if livinge, at Iron Gate, where the boats weekly come from Lee."

There is a world of silent and weary heartbreak in this and similar inquiries in the same letter.

When Mrs. Lake had come to New England, Charles I, Strafford, and Archbishop Laud were carrying things with a high hand, driving the Puritans out from the folds as if they had been wolves. Between that time and the date of Mrs. Lake's letter the commonwealth had risen, flourished, and, when the mighty man who gave it form had passed from earth, had fallen, and the Restoration, which all good subjects were bound to call "happy," had dropped a veil over things which it could not, and others which it would not, undo. Amid all their own troubles and overturnings, it is scarcely to be wondered at that the relatives left at "home" should sometimes have forgotten to write to their kin beyond the sea, from whose thoughts they were never long absent. The river of death could hardly have sundered chiefest friends more effectually than did the turbulent Atlantic then, but the hungry heart would still hope and cry out for certainty.

When John and Hannah Gallup happily planned and stoutly built their forest homestead on the banks of the little Mystic River, it well may be that they "laid its foundations in the feare of God and reared its walls in the terror of the Indians," as Samuel Smith of Hadley, Massachusetts, expressed it when writing in his old age in regard to the erection of the first meeting-house in Wethersfield, Connecticut, of which his father was pastor; and Samuel could speak feelingly upon the subject, having himself, in his young manhood in Hadley, had frequent occasion to defend his own house from savage attacks. Reverence for God was a part of the inheritance of the Puritan settlers, and terror of the Indians was a very natural consequence of their situation. Whoever may have been to blame in the first instance, there is no doubt that by fifty years after the landing at Plymouth, the question of proper treatment of the Indians received but one answer from the colonists: " We must extirpate them or they will exterminate us." At our distance from all such apprehensions it is easy to see the faults of the white men, and to sympathize with the misused Indian he was displacing; but had we lived in that time and under the same circumstances, it is doubtful if we would have been more altruistic than were our sorely harassed ancestors. The red man may have been as unjustly as he was unwisely treated by the white: but he was savage; he was untractable; he was cruel; he was treacherous. If his provocations were great, his vengeance was terrible. His vicinity was an unending menace to the home of every settler.

The celebrated "Great Swamp Fight" of 1675 was so called to distinguish it from the smaller Swamp Fight, which occurred at almost the other extremity of Connecticut in 1637. In the later of these battles the power of the truly great chieftain, King Philip, and of the native tribes of New England was forever broken. Perhaps, yes, even probably, this decisive fight might have been rendered unnecessary had gentler counsels prevailed thirty or forty years before, but by 1675 it had become inevitable.

When the colonial forces assembled to attack King Philip's fort the members of the opposing parties were supposed to be about two to one in favor of the Indians, full half of whom were supplied with muskets as well as with their native weapons; besides this, they fought behind defenses which, as the assaulting party had no cannon, must have seemed to be almost impregnable. The Narragansetts were the most nearly civilized of all the New England tribes. This fort was of their construction and was well built, with a strong and high palisade in the midst of a vast pine and cedar swamp. As an additional protection, the palisade was surrounded by a defensive hedge of interlacing felled trees, several feet in height and about a rod in thickness. Both parties to the conflict felt that they were fighting for their families, their homes, even their very existence as nations in these wilds.

The second John Gallup had always maintained pleasant personal relations with the Indians of whatever tribe, possessing those qualities of justice, firmness, and kindness which win confidence; but the moment was not one for considerations of this sort to have weight with either side. The husband of Hannah Lake was no longer a young man, having been married for thirty-two years; but the hardy pioneer was always in his prime between fifty and sixty, and age had bowed neither the back nor the spirit of Captain Gallup. At the head of his company of eighty men, he led an assault upon the fort's only vulnerable point, which was a reasonably well protected and gallantly defended gateway, where he fell with twenty of his men.

Whether his body was brought home to the woman who had loved him so long and so truly, I do not know, but probably it was not. The December weather was bitterly cold, the half-frozen morass was extremely treacherous. The victorious party had already marched twenty miles that day, fought fiercely, sustained only by scant rations of frozen food, and had the same distance to walk back again, carrying more than one hundred and fifty wounded men with them, so it is probable that the bodies of the slain were hastily interred on the spot where they fell.

Neither do I know how long the wife survived her husband; but I do know that the name of the hero-sire who fell in defense of his wilderness home was long held in reverent remembrance by his descendants. In a journal letter kept by his great-great-granddaughter, Juliana Smith of Sharon, Connecticut, I find this entry:

"This evening my Mother has been telling me about her great-grandfather, Captain John Gallup, who was killed in King Philip's War. I thank God to be descended from such a man. Truthful, Kind and Brave!"

CHAPTER V

TWO HOUSES IN OLD NEW AMSTERDAM

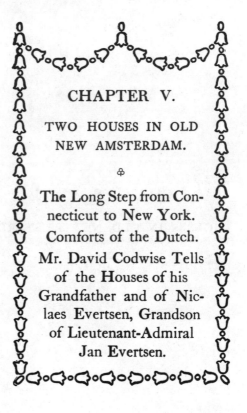

CHAPTER V.

TWO HOUSES IN OLD NEW AMSTERDAM.

♣

The Long Step from Connecticut to New York. Comforts of the Dutch. Mr. David Codwise Tells of the Houses of his Grandfather and of Niclaes Evertsen, Grandson of Lieutenant-Admiral Jan Evertsen.

IT is a long step both in time, in distance, and in customs from the pioneer home in New London, Connecticut, started in 1644, to the homes of prosperous Dutch citizens of New Amsterdam in 1698.

Material progress in all the colonies had been enormous during the years that had intervened. It has always been believed that the Dutch settlers were at no time subjected to the hardships that had been so grievous to the Pilgrims and their immediate successors, but that may have been a mistaken notion. Early Dutch records not having been so thoroughly searched, and letters, if any are in existence, being in a foreign tongue, we have been content to accept the conditions of later days as characteristic of the earlier ones as well. This much we know, that times were comparatively easy when Niclaes Evertsen, a recent immigrant from Holland, perhaps by the way of the West Indies, married Margrietye Van Baal, a native of the trading-post which her father had known as Fort Orange, but, which, eight years before her birth, had been obliged to take the English name of Albany.

Yes; times were not hard in the little city of New York, notwithstanding that it had been captured by the English, who were by no means as gentle and careful nurses of their colonies as the Dutch had been. The marriage just referred to occurred in 1698, at which time there was a considerable degree of material prosperity.

The Hollanders were natural traders, industrious, thrifty, honest, and persevering. Probably no nation had fewer vices or more virtues, and the last were of the kind that bring prosperity in their train. The English government paid them comparatively little attention, and the shrewd Dutch colonists took no pains to awaken the interest (or cupidity) of their new and undesired masters. In preserving a salutary obscurity they were undoubtedly aided by their quiet ways and their language, which few Englishmen cared to learn.

New York was now the little city's name upon colonial maps; but New Amsterdam it still remained in the hearts of its citizens, as well as in its customs and its people for many years to come. The British had been in possession for about thirty-five years when Niclaes Evertsen built his broad-roofed stone and shingle house somewhere upon the big farm which is said to have stretched from what is now Fourth Avenue, between Union and Madison squares, to the East River; but Dutch was still the language of the people, in Dutch were their records kept, and Dutch were all their tastes and ways.

The very first comers among the Dutch settlers must, like the New England and all other pioneers, have lived in huts of rough, or at best of squared, logs; but instead of being treated with biting neglect like the colonies of England, the Dutch received every possible aid and comfort from the government of their mother-land, and stores and supplies of all sorts were sent out to them as rapidly as possible and with a liberal hand, so that they were supplied with the comforts of those days sooner than their neighbors.

Even had the English so desired, they could not have given to their colonies as many comforts as could the Dutch, for the latter were far in advance of the former in all the peaceful and domestic arts. In addition to the help which they received from the home-land, the Dutch were fortunate in being most advantageously placed for acting as " middlemen " between Holland and the native American tribes, and thus they rapidly accumulated property ; hence their dwellings speedily became seats of comfort, or even of luxury, as those terms were then used.

The late David Codwise, for many years a master in chancery in the city of New York, dying in 1864 at the age of eighty-four years, was the husband of a sister of my grandmother. Under their most hospitable roof many of my girlhood's happy days were spent, and not the least happy were the hours passed in listening to my dear great-uncle's descriptions of the ways and things in old New York. Of his many talks I took some notes, and I am now extremely sorry that I did not take more, though I have been able to glean supplementary information from the many letters, wills, and expense-accounts now in my possession and relating to the periods of which he told.

I do not now remember whether the first of the two houses which Mr. Codwise described to me in considerable detail had belonged to his maternal or paternal great-grandfather; I think, to the latter. Its date, set in small red tiles in the yellow brick walls over its principal door, was A.D. 1700. This house, my uncle said, was the duplicate of one which was erected at or about the same time by his ancestor's partner and most intimate friend, Captain Niclaes Evertsen. The latter was the grandson of the Lieutenant-Admiral Jan (or Johan) Evertsen, a knight of the Order of St. Michael, and one of the most famous officers of old Holland's famous navy, to whose harvest of heroes his family had, in the course of less than a century, supplied, besides himself, no less than three vice-admirals, one commodore, and five *scheepsbevelhebbers* (ship-commanders). At least seven of the nine died in battle. Jacob de Liefde, in his book on the "Great Dutch Admirals," says that fifteen of the Evertsens had borne the name honorably in battle both on land and on sea, and one must wonder that the immigrant Niclaes was content to remain a merchant and captain of one of his own ships, peacefully trading between New Amsterdam and the West Indies. But times had changed. Holland and England had become friends, and the claws of Spain and Portugal had been too closely clipped to be longer dangerous to their enemies. So to Captain Evertsen in the new land his title had acquired a purely peaceful significance. That his business was profitable is proved by the estate which he left, and by the generous plenishings and furnishings of his unusually large and commodious house.

Among the notes which I took from Mr. Codwise's conversations I am glad to find a description and a rough plan of the ground floors of what were in their day considered two of the finest dwellings on the island of Manhattan. They were built at about the same time — after the same design and probably by the same workmen — for two men who were partners in business and attached friends — Captain Niclaes Evertsen, and the ancestor of Mr. Codwise, whose surname may have been either Codwise or Beeckman, as that was the maiden name of my great-uncle's mother.

The Codwise house stood on what is now Dey Street, where it was still considered a handsome residence, until destroyed by fire not long before my great-uncle's twentieth birthday.

Land on Manhattan Island was not then sold by the inch, and these two houses were built with a glorious contempt of economy of space. In the center of each rose a great chimney-stack of stone, having four immense fireplaces, each striding across the corner of a wide, low-ceiled, broad-windowed room about twenty-two feet square. On either side, beyond the four rooms thus grouped around the chimney-stack, were two others of about equal dimensions, each having its own fireplace, for two more chimneys rose, one in each gable-end of the houses. The first story of the Evertsen house was built of stone; that of the Codwise house was constructed of buff-colored brick imported from Holland — a needless expense, as Mr. Codwise used to say, because brick-making was one of the earliest and most successful industries started in the new land.

In both houses the exterior walls of the upper stories were covered by overlapping cedar shingles, clipped at the corners to produce an octagonal effect, as one may see them in certain cottages of to-day. In front and at the gable-ends the second stories projected a little beyond the lower. At the rear there was but one story, the long roof sloping from the peak by a slightly inward-curving sweep till it terminated over the low, comfortable-looking stoep, upon which opened the rear windows and doors of the first floor. All the first-floor rooms were handsomely wainscoted, and these, as well as the heavy ceiling beams, were, as Mr. Codwise remembered them, cased and painted white. Each fireplace was surrounded by borders of tiles, all illustrating scriptural or naval scenes, save one set, which, in reddish brown figures on a white ground, portrayed the adventures of Don Quixote. One of these last tiles I saw in Mr. Codwise's possession in 1860. The walls of one room in each of the houses were hung with embossed leather, which had once been richly decorated in arabesque designs, and even in my great-uncle's remembrance the gold tracings had not been badly tarnished. Other walls in the best rooms of both houses were hung with a very substantial sort of paper, pictured with sprawling landscapes in which windmills, square-rigged boats, and very chunky cows figured prominently. This was said to have been put on soon after the houses were built. According to the custom of the time, the bedrooms were always washed with lime.

On the second floor there were six rooms across the front, extending to the center of the house. The rest was left unceiled — a big open garret with square windows at each end and dormers along the sides of the roof, which sloped from the peak to the floor. In this great garret flax-hatcheling, wool-carding, and weaving went on almost without cessation, save in the very coldest weather,

7

when the looms were abandoned to the companionship of the rows of smoked hams hanging from the huge beams, the long ropes of sausage-links, the festoons of dried apples, and all the other stores which could endure the winter frosts. Those that could not do this were safely packed away in the dim recesses of the deep cellars which ran under the whole house. The latter was ventilated during the summer by leaving open the low doors, which formed a sort of sloping roof, covering the stone steps leading from the outer air on all sides of the house to the deeps below. In winter these doorways were filled in with straw and dried leaves, while earth and sods were laid over the closed doors in order to effectually exclude the frost. After this was done, late in the fall, the pitch-dark cellars could only be entered by the interior stairs.

The diamond-paned and leaded window-sashes had originally been brought from Holland; but by the time Mr. Codwise could remember them, all but a few had been replaced by other sashes filled with nearly square panes, twelve to each sash. This glass was so full of knots and streaks that no object seen through it appeared to be entire, but to be broken into disjointed parts. The glass of the imported diamond-shaped panes was much clearer.

At what time the Evertsen house was taken down, or whether it was burned, I do not know, but believe it to have been burned a few years before the Codwise mansion. After the destruction of each of them Mr. Codwise said that in the center of the central chimney-stack, which remained standing like a strong tower in the midst of the ruins, was found a small, diamond-shaped chamber, across the longest diameter of which two men might have lain down side by side. The floor of this chamber was of brick, and its side walls were the stone backs of the four corner fireplaces. Ceiling it had none, for the walls of the flues sloped inward as they rose, until at the top of the stack there was only a comparatively small opening, through which the noonday sun might send a blinking ray to cheer the floor beneath, or rain or snow might pitilessly descend. The little chamber was entered from opposite directions by two strait doors which formed the backs of two of the eight narrow closets flanking the four fireplaces. Good and secure hiding-places these chambers were, whether for men or for treasure. My uncle said that his father had seen the one in their house used for both purposes during our Revolutionary War, and to oblige both Tories and patriots; for his ancestors, whether the paternal Codwise or the maternal Beeckman, had maintained a strict neutrality, and were able sometimes to extend a measure of protection to personal friends in either party in their times of need. It is needless to say that the cautious heads of the families did not confide the secret of the chimney-stack to many persons. In summer this hiding-place must have been rather damp; but in winter, when the fires were burning in all four of the fire-places which surrounded it, it may not have been an altogether uncomfortable refuge.

A long, covered passageway led from one end of the stoep to a corner of the kitchen, which then, as is still usual in our Southern States, was in a detached building. Beyond it, again, stretched away the negro quarters, built sometimes of logs and sometimes of brick or stone, and mostly of one story in height. At right angles with these were the barns and stables, low, but exceedingly broad; also a blacksmithy, where horses and oxen were shod and repairs made, and a carpenter's shop. Taken together, the outbuildings made three sides of a hollow square in which were the milking- and feeding-yards. All this, of course, was on the farmstead of the Evertsens. The owners of the Dey Street house were merchants only, and had no outbuildings save stables for a pair of horses and a cow or two. It must be remembered that nearly all well-to-do citizens kept cows enough to supply at least all the milk for family use until the very latter part of the eighteenth century.

Neither of these houses followed the common Dutch custom of standing with gable-end to the street. Both opened from the center of the two-

story front almost directly upon the scantily trav-
eled highway, but at the rear were surrounded by
fruit-orchards and large gardens, wherein great
square beds of vegetables were edged by borders
of box or of flowers, as the case might be — for
your true Dutchman is not confined to strict utility, but is a flower-lover and cultivator all his
days.

A peculiarity of both houses was that the only
closets were those which flanked the fireplaces or
surmounted the high and narrow mantels. Great
carved chests of hard woods and massive mahogany
structures of drawers, or combinations of shelves
and drawers, were to be found in nearly every
room occupied by the members of a wealthy
Dutch family. Apparently clothes were never
hung up, but always laid away at full length in
these and similar receptacles.

In a large old mahogany wardrobe which once
stood in the Evertsen house, the three drawers
which form the lower half are very deep. The
shelves which form the upper half are equally
deep, and shove in and out like drawers, only without fronts, while broad doors close over them.
The wood still shows its beautiful grain, though it
has turned almost black with age, while the artis-
tically cut brass of the handles and escutcheons
responds to the labor of the polisher as brightly as
it could have done two centuries ago.

Among other articles which once stood in the

old Evertsen house is a tall mahogany structure
apparently designed for many uses, whose five
long and shallow drawers might have held its
owner's coats and breeches of satin or velvet, his
long silk stockings, his fine linen shirts frilled with
costly laces, and even his voluminous wig. In
the center, behind a leaf which turns down to
form a desk, is the little bank of pigeonholes for
holding filed papers, just as we see them in more
modern desks, only that among them are secret
receptacles for private papers, and two slides
which, when drawn out, were intended to support
candlesticks in such a way that the never too brilliant candle-light should best fall upon the desk's
contents. Above the pigeonholes, behind the
doors of mahogany, rise broad, deep shelves which
may have been used to hold books or clothes or
bed- and table-linen. To my mind, the varied
divisions of the shelf-space are not so suggestive
of literature as they are both of the linen of the
housewife and of the tall ledgers of the prosperous merchant, with long accounts to keep between
the traders of the interior, his correspondents in
the West Indian islands of Tobago, St. Thomas,
and Santa Croix, and with the merchants and
manufacturers of Antwerp and Amsterdam.

Though few books have descended to us from
the ancestral homes of New Amsterdam, it does
not prove that their owners were any more illit-
erate than the settlers of the other colonies. The

change of language from Dutch to English would
account for the natural disappearance of many of
the Dutch books. I know of one sacrilegious
creature who admits that about thirty years ago
she destroyed some forty Dutch volumes which
she had found in a garret of a house which her
husband had inherited, "to get them out of the
way, though the bindings of some were so pretty
it was almost a pity."

A serpentine sideboard of mahogany finely
inlaid with satinwood, now in the possession of
one of the Evertsen descendants, is believed also
to have stood in this house. It is known to have
descended through six generations to its present
owner. Sideboards there must have been here,
for there was much silver and china, scattered pieces
of both of which still remain. It is said that there
was little of the latter sold in New York city
prior to 1730. However this may have been, it is
certain, from the quantities that were bequeathed,
that wealthy residents owned much china long
before that date. Canton china was privately
imported at a very early period.

Not far from the present abiding-place of the
curiously decorated and really beautiful escritoire
above described is a mirror in two parts, the
smaller about one quarter the size of the larger,
the whole, with its frame of mahogany and the
carved figures of gilded wood which surround it,
being about six and one half feet in height by two

feet in width. The glass is said to be of Venetian make, and is still remarkably clear. So is that of two oval mirrors set in frames of beautifully cut brass, bearing on each side girandoles for three candles. The last two mirrors have been presented to a historical society.

Dining-tables with many slender legs, bed-steads, both of mahogany and of black oak, each with four high posts and deep side pieces, all richly carved, but too thick to be graceful, and cabinets curiously inlaid with ivory and tortoise-shell, stood in both of these old houses, and some of the fine pieces are still in existence. Tradition associates all the things we have particularly mentioned with the old Evertsen house; but they may not have belonged to the first Niclaes and Margrietye. Many of them were probably added by their son, the second Niclaes and his wife, Susanna Reuters, the great-granddaughter of the famous Admiral De Ruyter, who had many a time fought side by side with the Admiral Evertsen who was her husband's great-grandfather. The two old sea-kings had not always been agreed in regard to the best way to serve their fatherland; but both of them were true patriots and grand men, and did justice to each other's honesty and capacity, so we may imagine that they would have blessed the union of their descendants.

One possession which the first Niclaes must have guarded with the most jealous care, perhaps keeping it hidden in the secret strong room, was the silver-hilted sword presented by the state of Zealand to his grandfather, the brave old Admiral Jan Evertsen. The hilt of this sword, then broken from its blade, was seen in Poughkeepsie, New York, by my father when he was a boy of about fifteen, that is, in 1825 or 1826. It was then in the guardianship of a Mr. Richards, who had married a daughter of Nicholas Evertsen, the third of his name in this country, and a great-grandson of the first Niclaes. Upon the hilt was a handsomely engraved inscription in the Dutch language, which, unfortunately, the greatly interested boy could not understand; but he well remembered the names and date. The latter we do not now recall; but my brother, Gilbert Livingston Smith of Sharon, Connecticut, my sister, Mrs. Robert Clinton Geer of Brooklyn, New York, and I have all heard our father relate the incident and describe the hilt and inscription too often not to have them impressed upon our memories. The date upon the sword-hilt must have been previous to 1666, as that was the year in which the old hero died, fighting against England in a naval battle of four days' duration, on the first day of which his brother Cornelis, also an admiral, had perished. The hilt, my father said, was very heavy, and the size such that it could only have been wielded by an unusually large hand. Almost all the men descended from the first owner of this sword have been very large and strong.

Mr. Codwise remembered having heard of this

weapon, and also had heard his father tell of a fine gold medal which Captain Niclaes Evertsen had shown to some friends in his presence when a boy — a medal which had been presented to Admiral Evertsen by, as he believed, the States-General of Holland.

What has become of these precious articles? Are they still in the possession of some branch of a family which has become scattered through several of the States of our Union? Or have they,— have they — shameful thought! — shared the fate of so many of what should have been cherished heirlooms, and lost their identity in the silversmith's hateful melting-pot?

As all old American families too well know, there came a time when, old ideals having slipped away like children's outgrown garments, it was long esteemed a weakness to have a care for heirlooms as such. During this most deplorable interval, how many invaluable ancestral relics were ignobly converted into spoons and forks! An uncle of my own — a man, too, who had more than usual regard for ancestral relics — within my own recollection caused five dinner-plates of beaten silver, dating from between 1600 and 1650, to be melted to make a large pitcher! The latter is indeed much more beautiful than the plates, which were as plain as pewter and not a bit handsomer, but I never look at it without regretting its existence.

CHAPTER VI

THE CARES OF THE HUYSVROUW

CHAPTER VI.

THE CARES OF THE HUYSVROUW.

Every Homestead a
Manufactory.
Slavery.
Good Providers.
Spinning and Weaving.
Soap and Candle Making.
Washing.
Bread and Yeast.
Butter Making.
Nursery Lore.

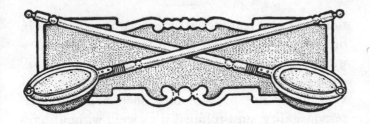

I T seems to have been the rule in all the colonies that the wealthier the settler the greater the amount of labor constantly carried on under his roof. There were no manufactories, and almost everything needed for household consumption or service had necessarily to be either imported or made at home. The *huysvrouw's* labors were by no means confined to the wise dispensing of the liberally provided stores. She and her daughters were happy and contented producers, as well as dispensers and consumers. If they did not personally scrub the uncarpeted floors, or build and feed the ever-devouring flames in the enormous fireplaces, or hatchel the flax, or card the wool, or weave the heavy stuffs for household use, or make the soap, or chop the sausage-meat, or dip the candles, or wash the linen—they had to know, as only experience can know, just how each and all of these things should be done, and also how to so marshal and direct their many hand-men and -maidens that the most and best work should be accomplished with the least friction. When reading, as one occasionally does in our day, of some " wonderful woman " who superintends a factory, or carries on some other line of equally active business, we should remember that very likely her grandmother once had as much responsibility, and fulfilled it as well, without having to go beyond the bounds of her own house to do so.

The days of the huysvrouws were also those of negro slavery, and they display all the best and some of the worst features of the system. If, on the one hand, the house-mistress were always sure of retaining the services of a well-trained and faithful servant, on the other hand it was by no means easy to get rid of one who was sulky, stupid, or careless. In fact, the servant question was as general a topic among the interested two centuries ago as it is now. Kings may go and Presidents come, and institutions may change like the weather, but human nature remains the same, and the diaries of from ten to tenscore years ago are found full of lamentations over the shortcomings of domestics.

Every farmstead of any pretension had to be, at the same time, a manufactory of almost all the things required for daily use. It is not probable that at the beginning of the eighteenth century there were many meat markets (or " fleshers ") to be found, even in the cities, and supplies of fowls and meat of all sorts save game were produced on the farms, where all that could not be economically disposed of while fresh was preserved by drying or spicing or salting or smoking for winter use. Several weeks of steady labor were required in each autumn to prepare the barrels of salted pork and of corned beef, to cure the scores of hams and sides of bacon, to prepare the miles of sausage-links, to try out and preserve the many stone jars full of lard so nicely that it would keep sweet the year round, to prepare the souse, the headcheese, and the rollichies. These last were made of chopped beef rolled in tripe and smoked. When desired for the table the little rolls were boiled and served cold, or fried and eaten hot. Besides all these, each in its proper season, were prepared stores of fish of various sorts, pickled, dried, or spiced, and great quantities of winter vegetables, as well as such fruits as could be kept for winter use by drying, or by preserving with sugar by the pound-for-pound method, so solidly sweet that the descendants of those who ate them must envy the grandparents' powers of digestion.

Of all the colonies, the Dutch were the most famous for these delicious (and indigestible) conserves. More than the others also did they distil and prepare an endless variety of cordials and fragrant waters for drinks or for flavoring to dainty dishes. Their mince-pies, fairly tipsy with their liberal allowances of hard cider or brandy, or both, their famous supplies of cookies, of crullers, of *olekoeks* (doughnuts), and of spiced cakes, were regularly made once or twice a week. Waffles, wafers, raised muffins, and griddle-cakes of various sorts were in daily tea-table use. Supawn, made of corn-meal boiled in water, salted and stirred the while with a wooden spoon till thick and smooth, took the place of modern cereals, and was served on every breakfast-table the year round. It was eaten either with butter and that good, old-fashioned West India molasses which no searching can now discover, or with milk. Sometimes, when the weather was too hot or too cold to make good butter, there was cream used, but usually this had to be saved to make butter; at the same time, skimmed milk would have been considered too mean a portion to offer to the cats. Dried fruits which had been previously soaked overnight were often cooked with and stirred through the supawn, giving an added flavor which was much relished.

The poultry-yard was every huysvrouw's pride. Even the wife of the importer, banker, or professional man living in the city kept flocks of hens, geese, ducks, and sometimes turkeys; but as the turkey was a notorious wanderer, and its eggs were not prized for eating, nor its feathers for beds, it was never very plentiful in the New Amsterdam poultry-yards.

Oysters and clams were brought in large quantities in the late autumn, and buried in beds of clean sea-sand, mixed with Indian meal, in the cellars, where they were profusely watered twice a week with water brought in tubs from the bay or river. In this way they were said to keep fat and good until the ice had broken up in the early spring, and the vast beds of native shell-fish which lay beneath the waters surrounding Manhattan Island were again accessible. It must be remembered that these waters were then frozen a great part of the winter, there not being sufficient traffic to keep the ice broken as now.

Game of all kinds, from deer to quails, was abundant for many years, and for at least twenty years subsequent to our Revolutionary War was both plentiful and cheap in the markets.

For many years there were no public bakeries, and the family bread-making was no inconsiderable toil. Even in the days of Margrietye Evertsen's granddaughters there was less yeast used than leaven. The latter is a lump of the latest baking buried in flour and kept in a cool, dry place until needed for the next baking. Numberless were the accidents which might happen to this. A degree too cold or a trifle too damp, and the leaven would not rise, so the bread was heavy; or a degree too hot, and the leaven would ferment, and so the bread was sour. If the sponge stood too short or too long a time, or its temperature was not just right, again there was trouble. If the big brick oven was under-heated, the well-made loaves would over-rise and sour before they were sufficiently baked, or they might be removed too quickly from the oven, and the half-baked dough would fall into flat and solid masses. If the oven was over-heated, the loaves would again be heavy, for the crust would form before the bread had had time to take its last rising in the oven as it should. The only wonder is that in those days there was ever any good bread; but the testimony is ample that among the Dutch huysvrouws good bread was rather the rule than the exception.

Probably the experienced cooks could never have told how they did it; but practice had made them so perfect that they knew to a second and a degree just the time and the heat required. A relative of my mother had married a wife of unbroken Dutch descent, and, with a tenacity characteristic of her progenitors in clinging to all old ways that had been proved to be good (and even, it must be confessed, to some that had not), she continued to use the old brick oven as long as she lived, and everything baked in it seemed to my childish taste to be perfection of its kind. She superintended every step of the long opera-tion, from the setting of the sponge overnight (with yeast, though, instead of leaven: she had been induced to consent to this innovation) to the removal of the sweet, light loaves from the oven sometime during the next forenoon. Full, round loaves of a brown so light as to be almost golden, I can see them now, standing in rows slightly aslant so that air could pass beneath, and covered loosely with spotless cloths of coarse linen, which last was as home-made as the bread, only not in her own time, but in that of her mother. Poor Auntie Aaltje (Aletta) would never have believed it possible, but after her death it was discovered that the dark-faced, white-turbaned old Chloe, who for so many years had patiently called her mistress to test the oven, and without a word (but sometimes with a covert smile) had accepted the patronizing verdict that "it would do," required no "superintending." But the huysvrouw who did not personally oversee all the important operations of housekeeping would have seemed to herself and to others to have failed in her vocation.

One of the most troublesome of all the housewife's duties was the quarterly soap-making. I can remember this function as performed at this house. Ugh! what a troublesome thing it was, and unsavory! For several weeks the "leach-tubs" stood in an outhouse filled with tightly packed hard wood-ashes from the big fireplaces, where wood was always burned during my kinswoman's life. The tubs, or rather big barrels, being filled to within about eight inches of the top with the ashes, were supported upon frames, beneath which stood small wooden tubs. Twice a day the vacant space left above the ashes was filled with boiling water. This, after it had slowly filtered through the ashes, became lye. Its strength was tested by an egg or by a potato about the size of an egg. If these would float about one third of their size above the lye, it was deemed strong enough; if not, it was poured through the ashes again; if found too strong, water was added.

When enough lye of the right strength had been collected, it was put into enormous iron pots and hung from the cranes over the open fire; and though my relative had come to endure a cook-stove for ordinary things, she always used the fireplace for making soap. The fragments of grease which accumulate in every household had been tried out while fresh, and reduced to cakes like tallow, only not so hard. These were now cut up and put into the kettles, apparently by guess. Then the boiling went on. If it was all right the soap would "come" in half an hour. If not, it might be many hours, or even days, during which water, or stronger lye, or weaker lye, or more grease might be added, also apparently by guess. The soap, when at last successfully produced, was in substance like a good, firm jelly; in color, a marbled brown; its odor that of a clear, clean alkali. It was very good for scrubbing and also for laundry purposes, though it must not be used too freely or it would yellow the clothes. It never made holes in them, as some of the modern sorts do. The husband was of Huguenot descent, and progressive in all things, so that the quarterly soap-making ended in his house after his wife's death.

This Auntie Aaltje was as decidedly Dutch in her ways as if she had been her own grandmother. While she lived there must no churn be used save the tall stoneware jar, perhaps the same one—at any rate, one probably just like it—which her old grandmother had caused her maids to fill to one half its capacity with good, rich, yellow cream, and place, according to the season, in a tub of ice-cold or of hot water. One of the maids meanwhile stood patiently beside the jar, plying the dasher up and down with rapid, even strokes until the butter "came." This also was done by guess; but if the huysvrouw's "guessery" was good—in other words, if she were an expert—the cream would have been skimmed and put into the churn at precisely the right moment and at the right temperature; then, in from twenty minutes to half an hour, the golden globules would have formed and gathered, and the butter would be ready to be skimmed out into a round tray of maple-wood, beautifully white, and made cold with well-water and "sweet with salt." Then with a water-soaked ladle the buttermilk was pressed out and salt added. This was the butter's first working. After a few hours it was again worked, and the next morning for the third time. The huysvrouw did not wash her butter. To extract the buttermilk she depended upon the conscientious muscular labor of her maids in pressing it all out. If this were not successfully done the butter would soon become rancid. The only wonder was that quantities did keep perfectly sweet and good, though very salt, from one June until the next. June and October were considered the best months for packing winter butter, the conditions of temperature and food for the cows being then nearest to perfection.

The custom of quarterly clothes-washings had been brought from Holland, and was long continued here among the Dutch settlers, notwithstanding that our summer heats, and the immense quantities of clothes necessary to maintain the state of cleanliness required by Dutch instincts and traditions, must have rendered it exceedingly inconvenient. As lately as 1760, we find in an old letter that "Grandmother Blum is so deep in her Quarterly wash this Weeke that she has no time only to send her love." The writer of the letter was a New-Englander married to a citizen of New York city, and the custom undoubtedly was strange to her. The washing was usually done in an outhouse called a *bleeckeryen* where the water was heated over the fire in immense kettles, and all the other processes of laundry work, conducted by the most laborious methods, were carried on there. This work usually required not less than a week, and quite frequently two weeks. During the three months intervening between these periods of cruelly hard labor, the soiled clothes had been accumulating from day to day in very large hampers of open basketwork, and stored in the bleeckeryen. It was this system of quarterly washings that rendered — and in parts of Holland and of Germany still renders — necessary the great stores of household and personal linens which are supposed to be brought to her new home by every bride, and for which the mothers begin to prepare almost from the birth of the first daughter. This preparation continued in the new land long after the custom of quarterly washings had given place to the much more sensible and sanitary custom now prevailing.

As the Grand Opera House in Paris was lighted with candles, affording certainly a dim if not a religious light, until sometime during the Regency, it is not to be supposed that lamps came into use in the far-away little city of New Amsterdam until a great many years later. In fact, there is little mention of the use of oil lamps in America before the middle of the eighteenth century. Wax candles were imported for festival occasions, but immense quantities of tallow candles were yearly dipped or molded for ordinary consumption. In all regions where the waxy and deliciously fragrant bayberry was plentiful, candles were made from it. When well prepared the wax was slightly translucent and of a light green in color. The snuff emitted so delicate an odor that on festive occasions, where many candles were burning, it was usual to blow some of them out at frequent intervals so that the room might be kept pleasantly perfumed.

The great dependence for cheerful light as well as for warmth in winter must have been upon the blazing knots of resinous wood dexterously distributed in among the slower burning logs of hickory, oak, and maple. By the blaze of these friendly fires there was seen much domestic happiness and much social enjoyment of a homely sort. The Dutch family relations were singularly close and intimate. Parental affection was especially strong and tender.

Among the descendants of old Dutch families here there still remain so many fragments of the nursery rhymes which used to charm the round-faced little Dutch lads and lassies that there must once have existed a copious literature of nursery lore. Part of one such jingle I can remember as my father sang it to my younger brother, who was a remarkably beautiful, black-eyed little fellow, then probably about two years old. I remember his teasing my father to play " trip-trop " with him. Then my father crossed his knees, and sat Willie astride of the suspended foot, holding him in place by the two hands. Then, swinging up and down the foot holding the delighted child, the rich, melodious barytone trolled out a catch of which I could only recall the first and last lines until the missing ones were supplied by Mrs. Vanderbilt in

her most interesting " Social History of Flatbush."
The completed rhyme runs :

" Trip a trop a tronjes.
    De vorkens in de boonjes,
    De koejes in de klaver,
    De paarden in de haver,
    De eenjes in de waterplass,
  So groot myn kleine [——] was."

Mrs. Vanderbilt translates this as follows :

" The father's (or mother's) knee a throne is.
    As the pigs are in the beans,
    As the cows are in the clover,
    As the horses are in the oats,
    As the ducks are splashing in the water,
  So great my little [——] is."

When the child's name was of more than two
syllables *poppetje* was substituted, this meaning
poppet, doll, or baby, a term of endearment. Several of my relations of Dutch descent used to call
me their " kleine poppetje." At the close of the
last line of the foregoing jingle the singer is supposed to toss the child as high as he can reach.
My father's paternal grandmother, from whose lips
he had learned the little Dutch jingle when a boy,
was born Margaret Evertson, and was a great-
granddaughter of the first Niclaes Evertsen.

To play " trip-trop " was always my little
brother Willie's bedtime entertainment by the open
nursery fire. So handsome and so happy were my
father and little brother, so impossible does it seem
to associate the idea of death with either, that even
now I cannot believe that they have joined the
other dear fathers and babies who played " trip-
trop " so many generations before them.

CHAPTER VII

THE ESCAPE OF A HUGUENOT FAMILY

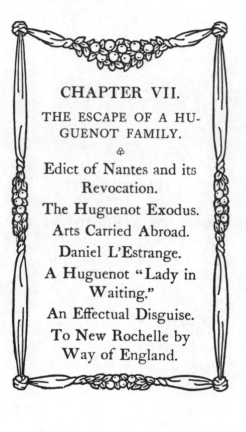

CHAPTER VII.

THE ESCAPE OF A HU-GUENOT FAMILY.

Edict of Nantes and its Revocation.

The Huguenot Exodus.

Arts Carried Abroad.

Daniel L'Estrange.

A Huguenot "Lady in Waiting."

An Effectual Disguise.

To New Rochelle by Way of England.

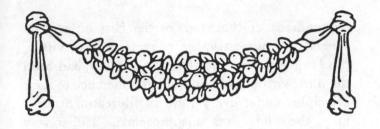

EVERY one knows of the French religious wars in the sixteenth century, and of the terrible massacre of St. Bartholomew, followed, after more wars, by the accession of " Henry of glorious memory," and by his promulgation, in 1598, of the celebrated Edict of Nantes. This edict by no means made all men equal before the law, but at least it granted toleration, as well as the most important of civil rights, and a measure of protection to the French Protestants. Almost as well known, but not so often brought to mind, is the long course of gradual encroachment on the rights conferred upon the Protestants by that edict. This encroachment never ceased until — long after the rights granted by the edict had been practically withdrawn — the edict itself was formally revoked, in 1685, by Louis XIV.

There is nothing in history more remarkable than the patience with which these constantly increasing and most odious persecutions were borne by the persecuted, except the fatuity which led to the final act of despotism, causing the expatriation of hundreds of thousands of the best citizens of France. If non-resistance to tyranny be a virtue, the Huguenots, for nearly half a century, had been the most virtuous of people. If adherence to their principles under every form of ill-treatment be a folly, their folly was unapproached. Either way they suffered for conscience' sake, and no people in the history of the world have exceeded them in this. Politically, the Protestant minority of the nation had no differences with the Catholic majority. All were alike loyal to the monarchical form of government and to the existing dynasty; there was no conflict of race or of province; and those of both the highest and the lowest social positions were to be found alike in the ranks of both parties. Religion was the sole ground of division.

In the decade preceding the Revocation of the Edict of Nantes, the exodus of the Huguenots from all parts of France had been great and continuous, in spite of the utmost vigilance on the part of the authorities. The numbers of the escaped have been variously estimated at from five hundred thousand to three millions. Some good judges think that about eight hundred thousand would be a conservative estimate.

In spite of his blind arrogance, Louis Quatorze was not so stupid as to wish to deport the best-behaved and most productive of all his subjects. He only made the mistake of supposing that he could command the minds and consciences as

easily as he could the arms and purses of his submissive people. To this end he determined to
buy heaven for himself by "converting" the
Huguenots to his own faith, and at the same time
to maintain the material prosperity of his kingdom
by preventing the escape of the many gentlemen
of landed estates, the bankers, the wealthy manufacturers, and the artisans who, at this time, composed the bulk of the detested party. Hence
every new act of persecution was accompanied by
additional precautions to prevent the escape of the
victims.

Most fortunate of all the Huguenots were those
who dwelt nearest the frontier. Under the terrible
and infamously effective system of the "drago-
nades," it is truly wonderful that such large numbers of the persecuted should have succeeded in
reaching places of safety; but the many are always
better than the few. Thousands of the refugees
long held in grateful remembrance the names of
their Roman Catholic neighbors who, often at the
risk of their own estates or even of their lives,
gave valuable assistance in the flight of their
Protestant friends.

No matter how fiercely might burn the anger
of the obstinate monarch at seeing the industries
of the Netherlands, Germany, Switzerland, and
Great Britain built up by those who had there
sought refuge from his own tyranny, he still had
the chagrin of knowing his best subjects to be

continually escaping from his clutches; and to-day the descendants of the Huguenots are among the worthiest and most enterprising of all the citizens of the countries which he most hated.

Many of those Huguenots who escaped to England subsequently came to her colonies. Although most of the refugees had been prosperous in France, and not a few had been wealthy citizens, comparatively few had been able to take much money away with them—the circumstances of their flight precluded that; but they all brought energy, industry, thrift, and power of endurance, as well as that truly delightful birthright of their nation, an invincible lightness of heart, while many of them also possessed skill in some hitherto peculiarly French handicraft, or in mechanical methods of unusual scope.

Like the Plymouth Pilgrims, the Huguenots came without any backing of national trade or class interest; but while the first came to preserve civil and religious rights which they were fearful of losing, the latter were involuntary exiles who, having already lost all rights, were flying for their lives, and were of all social grades, embracing a few noblemen, a larger number of *la petite noblesse* who would have been called "gentlemen com-moners" in England, and of professional men, merchants, bankers, manufacturers, and artisans, besides a comparatively small number of peasants. Of the last-named there were fewer than of the other classes, partly, perhaps, because it was impossible to escape from their enemies without the use of a great deal of money. Those who came were probably brought at the expense of the richer colonists, who expected to be repaid in labor.

Notwithstanding that the difference of their previous social conditions might have been supposed to prevent a strong feeling of unity among the Huguenot refugees, their "oneness of heart and mind" was from the first an object of wonder to the Dutch and English colonists, by whom they had been kindly welcomed. The persecuted were bound together by a common language, common perils, and a common faith. In their little settlement at New Rochelle there was for many years as near an approach to apostolic ways of living as has been seen since apostolic days. They were received most kindly by the earlier colonists, but they asked for no charity for even the poorest among them. All who had been successful enough in sending money out of France in advance of themselves, or had been able to bring any with them, placed their funds at the disposal of their chief men, to be shared as necessity required. It is said that they invariably cared for their own poor, and that these did not remain long in poverty, but were soon able to return all the sums which had been advanced to them by the wealthier members of the flock.

Some of the most flourishing of the hitherto

purely French industrial arts, such as the fine linen, silk, tapestry, and china manufactures, had been gradually carried to England, Germany, and Holland by the escaping Huguenots during the long years of persecution preceding the Revocation of the Edict of Nantes. Therefore to their brethren in these older lands the refugees in the new land sent for looms and other machines of better qualities than had hitherto been known here.

They did not have the capital to start their own industries on a large scale; neither did the British Colonial Office offer anything but discouragement for such undertakings; but every household became a little industrial colony, those who had never labored before now learning to do so with cheerful hearts.

The Huguenots were as sternly Calvinistic in their principles as ever were the Plymouth Pilgrims; but these principles did not seem to impart any bitterness to their natures. The little settlement in the colony of New York which they fondly called New Rochelle was from the first an abode of poverty and hardships most cheerfully borne. My dear mother's ancestry was very largely Huguenot, and from a few records of the traditions of her mother's family I have gleaned some fragments of interest which probably have a strong resemblance to the family histories of many others of similar descent.

In 1672 Daniel L'Estrange of Orléans, France,

was matriculated as a student of philosophy in the
Academy of Geneva, Switzerland, which at that
time was the only existing place where a French
Protestant could receive a liberal education in
his own language. The "pretended reformed"
were not allowed to have schools of their own in
France; nor, on the other hand, was it permitted
to them to send their children to the Catholic
schools without previously renouncing their own
and professing the national faith.

A few years later we find that M. L'Estrange
married Charlotte Le Mestre, also of Orléans. A
few years later still, the pair are residing in Paris,
where the husband is traditionally believed to
have been an officer of the Royal Guard—a tradition which seems to derive some support from
the fact that after his arrival in England he is
known to have held a lieutenancy in the Royal
Guard of James II. Strange as it may seem, many
Huguenots filled positions in the personal guard
of Louis XIV, where they were comparatively
safe from persecution, as their places were held by
a certain unwritten law of inheritance from the
days when Henry IV had filled its ranks, from the
commander down to the privates, with those upon
whose fidelity he could best rely; and these were
undoubtedly his old brethren in arms and in the
faith which political reasons had caused him to
forsake.

While her husband was in the Royal Guard,

Mme. L'Estrange was one of the ladies in waiting upon the dauphiness, Marie de Bavière, the gracious, studious, retiring, and accomplished daughter-in-law of Louis XIV. Thus the wife of the Huguenot was often obliged to serve her turn of duty at St. Germain and sometimes at Versailles. Although Mme. L'Estrange was well known to be of the "pretended reformed" faith, she was not molested, because she was a recognized favorite of the dauphiness. Perhaps the position of his wife at court combined with his own in the Royal Guard to save M. L'Estrange for a while from persecution, although he was known to be a determined, if not an aggressive, Huguenot; but the time came when he was obliged to seek safety in flight, and that, too, without seeing his wife. She was then performing her *tour de service* at Versailles; and her husband could only send her a verbal message, requesting that she should join him, with their child, and as much of their property as she could convert into ready money, at some designated point on the coast, where he would wait for her as long as possible, and whence they could take ship for England.

The person who was intrusted with the message either could not or did not convey it to the wife until many days, if not some weeks, after her husband's flight from Paris. I relate the story as I heard it from the lips of my maternal grandmother, who had heard it from her paternal grandfather.

Some of the particulars which she related are also given in Baird's "History of the Huguenot Emigration to America." I believe that the parts which rest only upon oral tradition are not less trustworthy than those quoted by Mr. Baird, which rest upon documentary evidence.

The husband's message was at last delivered, not directly to the wife, but to some one who conveyed it to the dauphiness. In spite of, or rather perhaps because of, her high position, the dauphiness was herself so closely watched that she had not the opportunity to transmit the husband's message safely until the hour of the *coucher*, which that night chanced to be particularly late. As the Huguenot lady was slipping the night-robe over the head of the dauphiness, the latter hastily whispered:

"In the cabinet at the foot of the stairs leading to my apartments, you will find one who will tell you what you must do, and do without a moment's delay." Aloud she added: "I am sorry you are suffering so much. You are excused from duty until I send for you."

A few moments later Mme. L'Estrange was in the designated cabinet. There she first heard that her husband had left Paris, she having for some time supposed him to be in hiding in that city, and also learned that, his flight having become known to the authorities, his property had been confiscated. The kind dauphiness had thoughtfully given a purse of money to the messenger, but it was not large, as she was not highly favored by her father-in-law, and had never very much cash at her command. The messenger had also two horses in readiness, and was ordered to accompany Mme. L'Estrange until she should have got safely started on her journey, under the care of friends whom she was expected to meet. But the dauphiness had apparently forgotten the existence of the child. The infant of two years was under the care of the married sister of Mme. L'Estrange in Paris, and thither the mother felt that she must first proceed, though the delay was well-nigh fatal to the success of her undertaking.

So well watched was every avenue of escape from Paris that several days were lost before an opportunity for leaving presented itself. One morning, before daybreak, Mme. L'Estrange disguised herself as a very poor woman seeking to go beyond the walls to glean food from the overladen market-wagons coming in. She carried her sleeping child in her arms. Her twin sister, dressed in all respects precisely like herself, followed at a safe distance. Arrived at the city gate, the mother begged to be allowed to take her child with her, but was not permitted; and it was only by addressing the sentry in his native patois of the Orléans country that he was induced to let the mother herself pass out, while he retained the child as a hostage for her return. Two hours later, while the awakened child was crying lustily, and the half-distracted sentry was busily looking for contraband goods in the market-wagons of the peasants, the aunt suddenly appeared, as if she had come in with the wagons, and claimed the child, which was gladly yielded to the supposed mother. Not for many years after did the true mother again see her child; but when he was grown he came to America, and married here. He it was who related the story to his son, the father of my mother's mother.

During several weeks after Mme. L'Estrange had escaped from Paris her adventures were many. When she finally reached the coast, it was only to find that her husband had been obliged to fly some time before. Her voyage to England was made inside of one of the very large casks in which the common kinds of wine were shipped to the whole-sale dealers in London. In similar casks more than sixty persons are said to have been shipped, at the same time, in the hold of the same small trading-vessel, whose English captain was liberally paid for running the risks attending such shipments.

During several years there were many hundreds, if not thousands, of escapes made in the same manner; and who can now imagine the horrors of such a voyage? The trip across the English Channel is not very welcome to the majority of travelers to-day, when not more than two or three hours are required, in vessels which, though bad enough according to our present standards, are princely compared with those of two centuries ago. In those days it frequently took a week to cross, and sometimes as long a time, or longer, was spent rocking at anchor, waiting for a favorable wind. Of course, the casks holding human freight were not hoisted on board until the latest moment; but whether waiting on shore in momentary peril of detection, or confined in casks on board ship, what an eternity must every hour have seemed!

With a small store of wine in a leather bottle, and some bread, a pillow or two, and such clothing as might be conveniently packed in with her, the wretched refugee was placed in the great cask, into the sides of which many small holes had been bored to admit air without attracting notice. The head of the cask was then secured in its place, and — carefully right side up — it was placed in the hold, where it was skilfully braced to prevent its being rolled about when the vessel was under way. My mother had seen, in the possession of one of her mother's brothers, a small pillow, filled with softly carded rolls of wool, covered with a stained and faded slip of brocaded silk, which was sacredly treasured because it had eased the buffeted head of the revered great-grandmother, when she was tossed about in her narrow prison in the hold of the blockade-running vessel on the uneasy waves of the English Channel.

Their " Red Sea " the refugees were wont to call

this Channel, though they certainly did not cross it
in the triumphant fashion of the hosts whom Moses
led from bondage to freedom. Some of the " cask
refugees " were found suffocated when their " arks
of refuge " were unheaded. Many more were se-
riously injured. The only wonder is that such great
numbers were taken from the French coast in this
way, and that so many escaped without more than
temporary injuries, before the persecuting authorities had discovered and put a stop to similar shipments. More fortunate than those who had to
cross the Channel were those who, like the ancestors of my mother's father, Bolden (or Bauldoin)
by name, were able to cross the frontiers into the
Low Countries. They had trials enough and hair-
breadth escapes by dozens, but their bodily sufferings were much less.

For the first few years after their escape M.
and Mme. L'Estrange fared comparatively well in
England, because the friends of the former had
procured for him a lieutenancy in the Royal Guard
of James II. But this monarch was not himself a
Protestant, and not too well disposed toward the
Huguenots, though state policy forced him to
receive them well. It was probably for this reason that Lieutenant L'Estrange, a few months
before James was forced to fly from his throne,
sold his commission, and, with the proceeds of this
sale and that of some jewels, came, with his wife, to
this country. Here he soon joined the settlement

at New Rochelle, and there and in New York city for many years he taught his own language to those Americans who wished to learn it, as well as gave instruction in the classical languages to boys who wished to enter Yale or Columbia (then King's) College.

At the same time, his wife, and later on their daughters, all of whom were born here, applied themselves to the new duties imposed by the new circumstances, in the cheerful spirit common to all persons who lead lives of faith and kindliness.

CHAPTER VIII

HUGUENOT HOMES IN NEW ROCHELLE

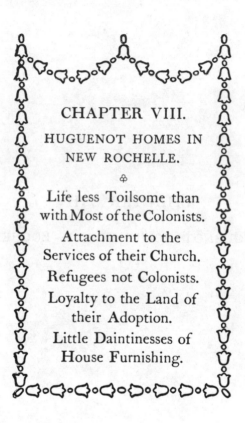

CHAPTER VIII.

HUGUENOT HOMES IN NEW ROCHELLE.

✿

Life less Toilsome than with Most of the Colonists.

Attachment to the Services of their Church.

Refugees not Colonists.

Loyalty to the Land of their Adoption.

Little Daintinesses of House Furnishing.

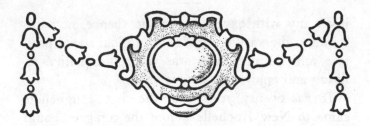

DAILY life in the Huguenot house-holds was probably less toilsome than in almost any others in the colonies. The refugees were too intelligent, industrious, and re-sourceful not to be able to escape many of the hardships of the very poor among the other colo.nists; and they were too poor to be oppressed by the multitude of anxieties and responsibilities inevitable to the rich citizens who then had to superintend the exercise of all sorts of labors under their roof-trees.

All of the very poor colonists must have had certain hardships to endure; but help of every sort was scarce, and sober and industrious persons were always sure of constant employment, while their tasks, like their lives, were of the simplest. At the same time, the home of every wealthy family was an industrial center. Thus there were no drones in either the richest or the poorest hives. The Huguenots, belonging to neither class, were in a sense coöperative. Neither the privations of the poor nor the multiplied cares of the rich fell

upon any with excessive weight; hence, notwithstanding the varying grades of original social position and culture, there was a great equality of
living and enjoyment among them.

It was twenty years after the first Huguenots
came to New Rochelle before the refugees could
spare the money to build a church or support a
pastor. The nearest place where religious services
were held in their own tongue was New York
city, twenty miles away; therefore, on every Sunday during the year, in fair weather or in foul, all
who were able to do so started very early in the
morning, that they might not miss the opening
prayer at 10.30 A.M. There were few horses
owned among the refugees, and fewer vehicles
of any kind. Such of both as they possessed were
devoted exclusively to the use of those who were
not strong enough to walk.

Many persons now living may still remember
Miss Isabella Donaldson, lately of Barrytown,
New York, as a person greatly interested in religious matters. She kept a scrap-book composed
of original communications concerning the hardships and trials of those who had come to this
country under stress of persecution. In this book
was a copy of a letter which was written about
1704 or 1705. I give this letter as I copied it in
1860 from Miss Donaldson's scrap-book :

"Every week I see the Huguenots pass the
house in troops on their way to their church in the

City. As they pass here all have lunch bags or baskets and also their shoes on their arms. Yet they are not bare-footed, for they are all provided with wooden shoes, such as the peasants wear in France and in the Low Countries. When they reach a stream not far from the church where they have erected a shed, they all stop and such of them as have other shoes change them before going on; the others wash their feet and their wooden shoes and put them on again. They are all very plainly dressed but some of them are very elegant looking persons with most charming manners. As they pass they are generally singing some of their psalms, that is, the psalms of David, translated into the French. Some of the airs are very grand and spirit-stirring, but many of them are as sad as dirges, and why should they not be? For surely this people have suffered much. Still they are nearly always smiling and happy. But to think of walking forty miles in going to and from church every Lord's Day! I am afraid my Christianity would never be equal to that."

For many years the conditions of life in New Rochelle, though not so bitterly hard as those of the Plymouth Pilgrims threescore years earlier, were very trying to those who had been gently born and tenderly nurtured in " sunny France," at that time the most advanced country in the world in the arts and luxuries of civilization. Perhaps that is not saying so very much, for luxury does not always, even now, include comforts, and at that time scant enough were what we now deem the most elementary comforts of life, even in the palace of the "Sun King" himself. In this country the French settlers, though originally among the poorest, speedily became distinguished by the amount of comforts, and even of luxuries, as these were then esteemed, which they gathered around them.

The homes of the earlier Huguenot settlers were, if one may judge by the two specimens which remain in New Rochelle, neither large nor fine; but they were substantial, and as comfortable as was possible under the conditions of the time. None in our country, save the families of high colonial officials, and a few of the very wealthiest of the colonists, possessed more of essential comforts than the French settlers at a comparatively early date were able to gather around themselves by dint of the industry, skill, and taste characteristic of their nation. There is a tradition that the first to utilize the remnants of worn-out garments by cutting them into strips and weaving them into floor-coverings were the French refugees. The rag carpet, as still sometimes seen, is by no means a thing of beauty, but in the days when the King of England himself did not always have a rug on which to rest his royal bare feet when stepping out from his lofty bed upon his chill and polished floor, the humble rag carpet would not have been esteemed an object of contempt even by his Majesty.

Among the earliest importations of the French settlers were spinning-wheels and looms of better quality than were previously known here. Immigrants from fruit-growing and wine-making districts of France brought grafts and roots, and succeeded in naturalizing most of the hardier varieties. A few were able to import hangings, mirrors, china, and furniture of rare beauty; but in general they possessed only those articles which could be manufactured here. However humble these might be in themselves, they would surely be made decorative by little touches which only the French hand could give.

Homespun linen yarn of heavy quality was by the Dutch and English colonists dyed and then woven into stripes and checks of varying degrees of ugliness for bed- and window-curtains. The French settlers used for the same purpose either purely white linen or that which had but one color. The preferred shades seem to have been a light blue, a sort of dusky green, and a subdued gold-color made by dyes of which they brought the secret with them. These linens, when made into hangings bordered by an embroidered vine or arabesque design in white upon the gold, or in gold and white upon the blue, or of varied colors upon the all white, were delicately beautiful, and became heirlooms in many a family, including that of my mother's mother. When this fashion was imitated by their Dutch or English neighbors, the "embroiderments" grew heavier, and, instead of being confined to simple designs, frequently became perspectiveless "landscapes with figures," wherein the yellow-faced shepherdess, clad in red and green, was taller than the stiff blue-green trees, and her black-and-white sheep were as tall as herself.

The bedroom of my mother's grandmother L'Estrange has often been described to me. The floor was painted as nearly as possible to match the subdued gold of the linen hangings. The ceilings and side walls were whitewashed with lime. The windows and dressing-tables were hung with tastefully arranged draperies, bordered with a grape-vine pattern embroidered in white, and further trimmed at the edge with a knitted fringe of white linen yarn.

The tall four-posted bedstead of carved mahogany was provided with a tester, with long draw-curtains, over which valances about two feet and a few inches deep, and cut into deep scallops on the lower edge, hung in a full ruffle from the cornice. Foot-curtains and all were of the same linen, all embroidered and edged with fringe in the same manner. Over the high and downy bed lay a fringed and embroidered coverlet of the same linen, only that in this case the vine was embroidered over the center part as well as the border. An immense stuffed chair, running easily on wooden globes the size of billiard-balls, which were the precursors of the modern caster, had a very high back and side wings, against which the head might rest. Such chairs were really comfortable, and some may still be found. This one had a neatly fitted slip-cover to match the draperies of the room.

The linen yarn for the draperies of this room was all said to have been spun by the first Mme. L'Estrange and her daughters, and it was afterward woven under their direction and embroidered by themselves. Until a comparatively late date there still existed other bits of their handicraft, in the shape of fans of peacock feathers, and humbler ones of goose and turkey feathers — these last decorated with painted flowers. There were also some hand-screens made by covering small hoops with tightly drawn slips of white silk, the joinings hidden by narrow fringe. One screen was embroidered with colored silks, others were daintily painted, and all were supplied with handles of carved or smoothly turned and polished wood. When a child I saw one of the peacock-feather fans (unfortunately, moth-eaten), and a pair of the prettily painted hand-screens. The latter were used to hold between the face and the blaze of the open wood fires, which, genial and delightful as they are, have a disagreeable way of scorching one's face and eyes.

Very graceful and delicately executed embroideries upon the daintiest of muslins are still shown which were made by members of this family, but possibly by those of a later generation. They are evidently from French designs. In the court of Louis XIV lace-making was an art cultivated almost as assiduously as that of embroidery. My sister and I now have a few yards of two patterns of lace made by Mme. L'Estrange, which happened to be trimming some part of her under-dress at the time of her escape from Paris. She taught the secret of its manufacture to her daughters, and for three generations her descendants made similar lace, though none was as filmy as that wrought in the boudoirs of Versailles, because it was impossible to get threads sufficiently fine.

The cultivated taste and the dainty arts brought from France made the homes of the Huguenots much more attractive in appearance than those of other colonists, even though the latter might be possessed of far greater wealth; and the same difference was manifest in their dress. The latter was certainly no more costly than that of most of those who had filled similar social positions in their respective mother-lands; but the Frenchwoman's fine eye for color, and her delicate skill with brush, needle, and bobbin, united to produce more attractive results. Similar touches of taste and skill appeared everywhere, and gave distinction to all the Huguenot homes, whatever may have been the

owner's social standing in the mother-land. As
neat as their Dutch neighbors, they devised labor-
saving methods to maintain perfect cleanliness
without being slaves to it. As liberal as the
English, they were far more economical, and by
their skill in cooking they succeeded in rendering
palatable and digestible even the coarsest fare.
Their skill in preparing rich dishes, sweet cakes,
and preserves was not equal to that of the Dutch
huysvrouws, and they could not compare with the
English in roasts and pastries; but in wholesome
dishes for daily consumption they far exceeded
both, and particularly in bread-making. It is traditionally related that the French were the first to
introduce the use of yeast in this country, the
larger part of all the colonists at that time, and
the Dutch for more than a century later, continuing to use leaven.

Perhaps the most keenly felt of the material
hardships which the French refugees had to meet
were caused by our stern winters and fierce summers, and the learning to subsist on the coarser
meats and vegetables which formed so large a portion of the fare of the English and Dutch colonists. Very soon, however, the refugees taught
themselves to resist or endure the extremes of the
climate, and, with their readiness of adaptation, they
learned to prepare even the coarsest foods with a
culinary skill which puzzled while it pleased their
new-made friends. It is a little curious to note

how long it was before the delicately flavored soups, the light omelets, and the delicious entrées, common to all Huguenot households, came to be adopted by even those who were the loudest in praise of these delicacies as made by the French ladies. Some special forms of buns and rolls excepted, very few of the distinctively French dishes appear to have been used in families not of French descent, prior to our Revolutionary War.

Notwithstanding all the invincible light-heartedness of his nation, the lot of the Huguenot must be felt to have been sad and lonely. The Puritan was an emigrant from his native land for conscience' sake, it is true, but his conscience was set upon political as well as religious rights. He came here of his own accord, that he might have freedom to worship God and govern himself (and others!) as he thought fit. The Dutchman, having achieved moral and political liberty for his hardly won and overcrowded dike-lands, did not feel that he was expatriating himself when he sailed for the New Netherlands, but rather that he was enlarging the Dutch domains. Even after he had fallen under English rule he did not greatly repine.

The Huguenot, on the contrary, was not a colonist, but a refugee. In all the world there is not a more truly patriotic nation than the French. They love their people and their homes, their customs, and their country's very soil with a passionate devotion. The Huguenot was no exception to the rule. For the privilege of continuing within the beloved borders of France he had gradually sacrificed his every political and almost all of his civil rights. Not until the only alternatives left were the denial of his religious faith, death, or flight, did he resort to the latter. Then he felt himself, not a voluntary emigrant from his native land, but an exile, an outcast; and his feeling toward the government which had sent him so harshly forth was of the bitterest description. This was shown in many ways. The French Canadian, a voluntary colonist, retains his language even to-day, though long cheerfully submissive to an alien rule. The Huguenot refugee ceased to speak his own language as speedily as possible. My grandmother and her many brothers and sisters were only the fourth generation in this country. As their own grandfather had been left behind in France and educated there, they might well be counted as the third generation here. Yet, with the exception of some of Marot's psalms, two or three childish rhymes, a proverb or two, and a few chance expressions, their speech betrayed no traces of their national origin. Though their great-grand-father, the refugee, taught his own language for several years, the household use of his beautiful mother-tongue was distinctly discouraged by him.

To the land of their adoption the Huguenots transferred to the full all the inborn loyalty of their characters. During Great Britain's long wars with

France — 1744 to 1763 — the descendants of the Huguenots, whether in England or the colonies, bore their part in continental or provincial armies, doing valiant and often highly distinguished service in both.   Many of the best Huguenot families in New Rochelle and Rye sent representatives to fight the French and Indians.   Among them were my mother's grandfather and his brother.   The first was also, when the time came, an officer in our Revolutionary army.

CHAPTER IX

HUGUENOT WAYS IN AMERICA

CHAPTER IX.

HUGUENOT WAYS IN AMERICA.

Alterations in Names.
Resentment toward their
Native Land.
Differences between
French and English
Calvinists.
Schools Established by
the Huguenots.
Amusements, and Games
of Courtesy.

THE utter abandonment by the expatriated Huguenots of all connection with France is shown in nothing more clearly than in the change of both christened names and surnames. Henri and Pierre, Jeanne and Marguerite, became Anglicized almost immediately, and, it must be confessed, not to their betterment. The spelling of surnames was apt to follow the pronunciation of their new friends and neighbors. Even when the spelling was retained the sound often became hopelessly altered. De la Vergne, though retaining the accepted spelling, was soon written as one word, and pronounced (think of it!) Dillyvarje. Often the spelling also was changed beyond recognition. Bonne Passe (Good Thrust; in the days when good swordsmen were valued this was a name of honor) first became shortened to Bon Pas, and then changed to Bunpas, followed by Bumpus and finally contracted to Bump! L'Estrange was first known as Streing, then as Strange, afterward as Strang, and even, in a few cases, was changed to Strong.

In writing the name of this last-named family I have followed the usage of at least some of its earlier members in this country, as well as a widespread belief among them all in its correctness. It is a family tradition that when the young Daniel — afterward the refugee — was sent to Switzerland to enter the academy there as a student of philosophy, July 29, 1672, his surname was purposely misspelled as Streing to avoid giving a clue by which his father's persecutors might discover whither the son had been sent; and that afterward, upon the young student's return to France, and during his stay there as a member of the Royal Guard, he had resumed his rightful name. But later, when he was obliged either to abandon his principles or to fly for his life, he thought it wise to again adopt the name of Streing for the sake of members of his family still residing in France; for, as is well known, the spies of Louis XIV were almost as active in London as in Paris, and though the refugees there could not themselves be reached by the laws of France, the tyrant's wrath at their immunity was often visited upon their relatives still unable to escape from his clutches. The change of name was considered of enough importance to be kept up even in this country until after the arrival here of the oldest son, whom his heartbroken mother, as before related, had been obliged to abandon at the gate of Paris. The son did not come over until he was twenty-one or

twenty-two years of age. By this time the habit
of the name had become fixed. This son seems to
have retained his name as L'Estrange, and some
of the others also used it, at short and irregular
periods. Both L'Estrange and Streing appear
to be names belonging to the numerous ranks of
the petty gentry.

Among the reminders of their native land to
which the refugees clung the longest was the version of the psalms of David by Marot—that version
so hated by the persecutors that every copy discovered by them was immediately treated with as
much animosity as was the Bible itself. Even
after the descendants of the refugees had so far
forgotten their ancestral tongue that they preferred
to read the Bible in English, they yet sang, to the
old melodies which had so often thrilled their
fathers' souls, the beloved psalms which were still
cheering the hearts of their persecuted brethren
hiding in the caverns of the Cévennes, where alone
the remnant remaining in France could worship as
conscience dictated.

I would give much if I could now recall the air
to which my mother's mother and one of her sisters,
both of them considerably over seventy years of
age at the time, tremulously sang the psalm in
which occur the words:

"Quiconque espère au Dieu vivant,
Jamais ne périra!"

But both the air and the rest of the words have escaped my recollection. What has not forsaken me is the memory of two petite but still remarkably handsome women, one of them very erect, the other a good deal bent, but both still vigorous of mind and body, as, in the late twilight of a summer Sunday evening, they sat together in a shadowy room and crooned the old sacred song with a strong and faith-inspired emphasis on *jamais*, stopping in a startled, half-ashamed way as soon as they discovered "Little Pitchers" trying to efface herself in a dark corner, because she well knew that the entertainment would end as soon as her presence should be known.

So far did some of the Huguenots carry their resentment to the government which had so unjustly expelled them that they did not like to be reminded of the land from which they came. It is told of one who lived for many years in Charleston, South Carolina, that while he never thoroughly mastered the English language, he would speak only in that tongue even within his own family circle. He had his name translated into its English equivalent, and though his accent invariably betrayed him as not of American or English birth, it was not definitely known by his neighbors that he was born in France until a short time before his death, when it became necessary to declare his nativity in order that he might obtain possession of some property willed to him by a relative in Burgundy.

Probably few of the refugees went quite as far as this, but certainly for many years their descendants, while rejoicing in the name of Huguenot, seemed to resent being called French. I remember that for some time my own grandmother (of the fourth generation in this country) opposed her grandchildren's study of the French language. One day I said to her, "But, grandmother, your own ancestors were from France, so the language is partly our own, and why should we not study it?"

Her large and brilliant black eyes flashed at me over the tops of her spectacle-bows as she replied: "Yes, they came *from* France. They did not remain there. France is now the home only of persecutors and atheists." And I fear that she was never able to believe that any one who could not be properly classed as either the one or the other could continue to exist in the country which had so pitilessly cast forth its most loving children.

This trace of resentment seems to have been the only somber characteristic of the Huguenots and their descendants in this country; and even this had its good side, for it led to their more ready adoption of the ideas and institutions of the new land which welcomed so warmly and so helpfully those who had "endured hardness" for the sake of their common faith.

Doctrinally, the Huguenots and the Puritans were the same. In practice there were many points of difference. The Puritan was a very strict Sabbatarian, beginning at sunset of Saturday a twenty-four hours of abstinence from any avoidable work, as well as from any pleasure save that which his devoutness found in religious services. The Huguenot Sunday began and ended as now. Like Calvin himself, the refugees did not think it essential to avoid all pleasant things on Sunday more than on other days, and all who had friends living near the wayside stopped in to visit them as they returned from church, for the Sunday time that was not devoted to church services and to an hour of catechizing at home was not considered as ill spent in cheerful social intercourse.

In Calvinistic Switzerland it had been customary to indulge — after church hours — in any form of innocent amusement. The Huguenots seem to have drawn the line just short of this. But on week-days their national light-heartedness was bound to display itself in as many ways as their circumstances would permit. Tableaux and little comedies were frequent, while dancing was the expected amusement in most households at every evening gathering, and these took place as often as possible. Children were instructed with a degree of gentleness and consideration quite in contrast with the sterner ways of their coreligionists of English or even of Dutch descent.

Cheerfulness, even gaiety, was the rule. A gloomy Huguenot was an anomaly to be pitied and apologized for by his compeers only on the ground of exceptional misfortunes. Yet, when one considers the horrible oppressions which they and their ancestors had endured without relief for almost a hundred years after the end of the temporary respite granted by the Edict of Nantes, one must wonder at, while forced to admire, their happy dispositions.

The "boarding and day schools for young ladies" which were established in New Rochelle were eagerly hailed by the elder English and Dutch colonists. Hitherto their daughters had had few educational advantages. The sons could have private tutors or attend fairly good preparatory schools which fitted pupils for the colleges so early established in the colonies; or — if his parents were among the magnates of the land — an especially fortunate youth might be sent to one of the great English universities. In general, the girls had to be content with the crumbs of knowledge which dropped from their brothers' not over-supplied tables, though, in some rare instances, governesses were brought from over sea for their benefit. So when these French Protestant schools were opened by those who had enjoyed every then prized advantage of social culture, they were well patronized from the start.

In these schools were taught not only the language of the "politest of the nations," — to employ the words of Lord Chesterfield, written half a century later, — but also all the "ladylike accomplishments" of the period. English teachers were engaged to instruct in the grammatical use of their own tongue, both written and spoken; but it may be imagined that this was not considered of nearly as high importance as the more showy accomplishments, which could be acquired at these schools only. Enough of music to enable a young woman to play a little for dancing (although the fiddle of some dance-inspired old African was usually preferred by the dancers), or to warble a few songs in her (presumably) fresh, sweet tones to the accompaniment of the probably thready or wheezy spinet; enough of French to enable her to read it easily, write it fairly well, and hold a not too monosyllabic conversation in that language, were certainly considered as very desirable accomplishments.

A still more serious business seems to have been "Instruction in the Arts." A few of the flower-pieces which were painted from nature in water-colors by some of the pupils of these schools are still preserved and are really beautiful. When on a visit to Nova Scotia some years ago, I saw several which had been taken there by some of the Royalist families exiled from here in 1783. They bore the inscription, "Eleanora Morris, Pension de Demoiselles de Madame De la Vergne, La Nouvelle Rochelle, Province de New York, 1736." The few still surviving landscapes which I have seen were stiff things not evincing much of talent on the part of the pupil, or skill on that of the instructor. The embroideries, as might be expected, were especially good. Occasionally a fine piece of Rochelle tapestry or bed-hanging may yet be found in the possession of fortunate descendants of some who once were New Rochelle pupils, and so may many specimens of exquisite embroideries on the most delicate of muslins, as well as remnants of laces which are known to be the handiwork of some of Mme. De la Plaine's or Mme. De la Mater's pupils.

But probably even more than all of these accomplishments, the principal thing desired for their daughters by the parents was instruction in "gentle manners" — the manners not only of persons who were of gentle birth, but who also had been so early taught by precept and example that their graces seem to have been born with them, a part of their very selves. The pupils were taught how to avoid all awkwardness of movement or carriage; how to bear themselves gracefully erect; how to enter a drawing-room with a grave and gracious inclination, seeming to include all who are present while addressed only to the hostess, and to leave it without turning the back, as one retires from the presence of royalty; how to graduate their greetings from the pleasant deference due to elders or social superiors to the sweetest condescension toward their juniors or social inferiors; how first to arrange, and afterward how to preside at, a handsomely spread dinner-table with dainty elegance and efficiency; and also how to dress themselves with taste and effect in the fashion of the day. Dancing was a matter of first importance. The "stately steppings" of the courtly dances of the period cost time, thought, and much careful teaching on the one side, and submissive labor on the other, before any pupil could be considered as a perfected scholar. Incidentally with all these things, a great deal of valuable instruction was given in the finer graces of courteous speech, and all that gentle consideration for others which is at once the flower and the root of good breeding.

From the first, the Huguenots, of whatever degree, seemed to have endeavored to transmit to their children the traditions of politeness which they had brought with them from France. For a long time — perhaps even yet it may be the case in some families of this descent — the children were taught some of the details of good manners by little games. These may have been invented in this country to supply a lack of more regular instruction, or they may have been simply adaptations of similar games once played in the motherland.

The only one of these *jeux de courtoisie* of which I have retained any distinct recollection conveyed instruction in the arts of courtesying and bowing, and was also a lesson in propriety. It was called "La Loi des Baisers." In this game only girls were allowed to play, One of them stood in the center of a room, and round her passed

a decorous procession of little women, each one
of whom bowed or courtesied low before the gracious "reigning lady," kissing her extended hand
and chanting:

"La main! La main, Jolie! Petite!
Pour les amis. Pour les amis."

To each the small lady in the center courtesied
with more or less of grace, and responded, the
friends in this case being supposed to be of the
opposite sex:

"Merci, merci; mes bons amis."

At the next round the "reigning lady" presented her brow to be kissed by all in turn, while
the chant now ran:

"Le front! Le front! Le noble front!
Pour les pères, et les frères."

To this the response was a lower courtesy and
the words:

"Mon cher papa! Mes frères chéris."

At the third turn of the procession the small
lady presented both her hands and her cheeks,
while the chanted words were:

"La joue! La joue! La rougeante joue!
Pour les douces sœurs, et les mères."

In this the kissing was mutual, and on both cheeks, without further words. At the fourth round the "reigning lady" was seated, demurely placing one small finger on her archly pouting lips, while the others passed by, each with half-averted face and one hand raised as if prohibiting a nearer approach, while chanting:

"La bouche! La bouche, si ravissante!
Pour les maris! Mais seulement les maris!"

The rounds generally continued until each little girl had played the part of the reigning lady.

It was a very old lady who taught this little game and its chanted words to several of us, little girls of ages varying from five or six to eight or ten years. At first we learned the words by rote only, just as generations of children have learned "Hickory, dickory, dock," but later on we grew to know the meaning, whether by the interpretation of older girls or not I do not now remember.

If any living descendants of Huguenots in America retain traces of others of these *jeux de courtoisie*, they should not fail to see that such traces are recorded. Too precious to be allowed to fade entirely away are these faint remains of the efforts made by the Huguenots to retain for their children, in the midst of the wilderness which had welcomed them, the graces and proprieties which had been birthrights in their old homes.

CHAPTER X

A COLONIAL WEDDING

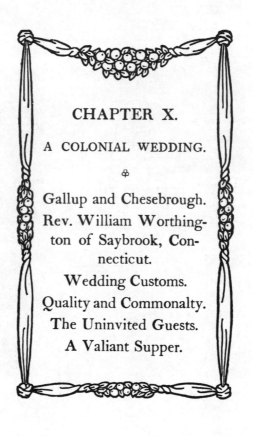

CHAPTER X.

A COLONIAL WEDDING.

Gallup and Chesebrough.
Rev. William Worthing-
ton of Saybrook, Con-
necticut.
Wedding Customs.
Quality and Commonalty.
The Uninvited Guests.
A Valiant Supper.

T HE year was 1726. The bridegroom was the Rev. William Worthington, then pastor of the church at Saybrook, Connecticut. The bride was a former parishioner in the town of Stonington, Connecticut, by name Temperance, daughter of William Gallup and his wife Sarah (Chesebrough), and granddaughter of Captain John Gallup and his wife Hannah (Lake), of whose "pioneer home" we have already read.

As known to all readers of colonial history, this Captain John Gallup, the second of his name, had been a man of much influence with the Mohegans, or friendly Indians, many of whom had followed his leadership in the Great Swamp Fight of 1675, in which he bravely fell at the head of his company. To his son, William Gallup, the Mohegans had transferred the allegiance they had given his father, and, in his turn, he continued to exercise over and for them the same sort of fatherly guardianship which they had received from Captain Gallup. A knowledge of this fact is essential to the comprehension of an incident of the wedding of Mr. William Gallup's daughter.

This family was among the most prominent and highly connected in what is now known as New London County, Connecticut, and in the theocratical régime of New England the minister always held the first rank by right of his office, as well as by the gentle birth and breeding which were usually his. For both reasons all the neighboring "people of quality" were naturally among the invited guests. The pastor, being in spirit as well as in name the father of his flock, could not allow any member of his late parish to be overlooked, though it probably embraced every soul in the township. To be both just and generous to all, it was decided to make a wedding-feast of two days' duration, and invite the guests in relays, "according to age, list and quality," in the same way that sittings were then assigned in many, if not all, of the "meeting-houses" of New England.

The first day of the feast was that on which the marriage ceremony was performed by the bridegroom's personal friend, the Rev. Ebenezer Rossiter, and not by a civil magistrate, as was the early custom in all the Puritan colonies. It is almost certain that there was no wedding-ring. Even as late as half a century ago these were rarely used by descendants of the Puritans. There were present on this day only the relatives and intimate friends of the contracting parties. As the bridegroom was a minister, no doubt all the neighboring clergy, and as many of their families as could come, were numbered among the friends on this day. So, also, were several of the highest colonial dignitaries, as appears by the time-stained chronicle, written nearly fifty years later, from the relations of her grandmother, the bride of that day, by Juliana Smith, a granddaughter of the Rev. and Mrs. William Worthington.

For the first day's feast long tables were spread with much profusion, and with what to modern eyes would seem like confusion as well. Soups were then rarely, if ever, served on occasions of ceremony, and all meats, fish, side-dishes, and vegetables were placed on the table at the same time, and served without change of plates. It was considered an "innovation" at this wedding-dinner that "coffee, pies, puddings and sweetmeats formed a second course."

The guests were seated with great regard to precedence. Probably there were not many chairs, for even in England "settles and forms" continued to be more commonly used than chairs in the best country houses at least as late as 1750. Such as there were — and probably every good neighbor contributed such as he possessed for this occasion — were carefully reserved for "the most infirm and the greatest dignitaries."

"Immediately after the asking of the blessing by the oldest minister present, tankards filled with spiced hard cider were passed from hand to hand down the table, each person filling his own mug or tumbler." A punch-bowl is not mentioned in this chronicle as having formed a part of the table furniture, and as it is expressly mentioned that the drinks were poured from the tankards into mugs or tumblers, it is probable that the custom, mentioned by Mrs. Earle in her "Customs of Colonial Life," of passing the punch-bowl from hand to hand for each person to drink from, had already become obsolete; indeed, it is not certain that such a custom was ever habitual among the better sort of colonists. Tankards were undoubtedly so passed, not only here but in the rural districts of England, as late as "in the days of good Queen Anne."

A very few of the tankards and mugs at this wedding may have been of silver or of glass, and still fewer of delft or of china, but where there were so many the greater part must have been of pewter, horn, or wood. Of these articles, as well of the chairs, it is likely that all the well-to-do neighbors contributed the best of such as they possessed, this generous sort of neighborliness being a characteristic of the time and of all new settlements. Articles of silver were not as plentiful in New England as in the other colonies, but by this date nearly all families of distinction possessed a few, and in spite of the natural losses by fire and other calamities, there are still existing some relics which ornamented this long-ago wedding-dinner.

A curious dish, which may possibly, even probably, have been used on that day, is still in possession of a member of the family connection, a descendant of the Chesebroughs. This dish is here
described in the hope that some one may be able
to determine what use it was originally intended to
serve. It is circular, about nine or ten inches in
diameter, perhaps three inches deep, standing upon
a circular base; it would hold from three to four
pints of liquid, and has a cover. So far there is
nothing to distinguish this piece of very ancient
red, yellow, and blue delft from many another
which we would not hesitate to call a vegetable-dish.
But, perched against one side of its interior, like a
swallow's nest under the eaves, is a pocket-like
thing that would hold three or four tablespoonfuls
of liquid were it not perforated like the strainers
of tea-pots. It has been stated — on what authority I know not — that when tea was first brought
to Holland it was served as a soup. Is it possible
that this queer old side-pocketed dish was made
for the infusion and serving of the new herb?

If there were not enough dishes of the better
sort to accommodate all the guests entitled to
them, preference was always, at such entertainments, given to the older persons present. The
juniors would be served on this first day, as all
would be on the next day, with dishes of brightly
polished pewter, or in trenchers of maple, tulip, or
poplar wood, scoured to an almost snowy whiteness.

There would be few spoons of silver, but many made of pewter or horn; no silver forks, and perhaps not an oversupply of steel ones. Among the relics in the old house at Sharon are still preserved half a dozen specimens of an implement which preceded forks — sharply pointed bits of steel, about four inches long by an eighth of an inch in diameter, set into handles of bone. When I first found them and took them to my grandmother with a " What *are* these ? " she laughingly told me to " guess." I thought they looked more like ice-picks than anything else, but she assured me that they were the precursors of forks. They must have performed their office but " indifferent well," though, as an improvement upon fingers, some of them may likely enough have been used on this occasion.

Some of the pewter dishes now cherished by the descendants of those who, as relatives or friends, were present at this wedding, are marked with the owner's initials as carefully as if they were of silver. Indeed, a full set of pewter tableware was considered a fine wedding-gift from a father to his daughter. A pewter porringer, belonging to the family which owns the dish of ancient delft mentioned above, is a really pretty thing, graceful in shape and having a fancifully cut flat handle projecting from its side. It is recorded that in Queen Elizabeth's time cocoanut-shells were used as drinking-cups, being polished, and set sometimes in silver, and sometimes in pewter. In the colonies polished cocoanut-shells were also occasionally used as ladles, having long handles of polished wood attached to them. At least one such ladle still exists. It has a prettily fashioned handle of maple wood. Its exact age is not known, but it or its counterpart might well have been used at this wedding-feast.

On the first day of the feast, besides the preliminary draught of spiced cider, there was brandy for those who craved it, and much good Burgundy and Madeira for the more temperately inclined. Three casks of Madeira (size not mentioned) are recorded as having been broached on that day.

On the second day the "commonalty" began to assemble at about nine o'clock in the morning. (The "quality" on the previous day had waited until eleven.) The tables were served to successive guests during the day. Foreseeing the demand, all the good housewives in the vicinity, with their servants, had been assisting Mrs. Gallup and her servants in the preparations, and afterward, with neighborly coöperation, they assisted in the serving of the stores of good things.

On the first day, "after the removal of the substantial part of the meal, the ladies left the table, the table cloths were removed, and various strong waters, together with pipes and tobacco, were brought on, in company with trays filled high with broken blocks of nut-sweet." This last was a highly prized candy made from maple sugar made soft with water, placed in a shallow iron pan over the coals, with a liberal allowance of unsalted butter, and slightly scorched. While scorching, the blanched meats of hickory-nuts and butternuts, or sometimes almonds when this foreign dainty could be procured, were added with a liberal hand. When cooled this became firm, and was esteemed "equal to anything in England."

On the second day this regular order of things, with the customary toast-drinking, was manifestly impossible. "As each relay of guests left the tables they passed out of the front door near which stood an immense Bowl, long ago hollowed out by painstaking Indians from a bowlder, for the grinding of their corn. This was filled with Punch which was ladled out freely to all who presented anything from which to drink it, while great piles of powdered Tobacco and a good bed of coals to furnish light, were free to all who had pipes." This punch, whatever liquor might have furnished its body, was sure to have been well seasoned with the best of West Indian sugar and lemons, for there was already a brisk trade between the Connecticut coast and the West Indies, and at this time of the year the trading-vessels would have been coming into the home ports.

This unique punch-bowl held many gallons, and it speaks well both for the temperance of the guests and the good quality of the liquor provided, that "no one became boisterous, though the big Bowl was kept well and strongly replenished during the entire three days of this wedding feast." For three days there were, though only two have yet been mentioned here.

Early—very early—on the morning of the second day, almost before the active men- and women-servants had opened their eyes upon the heavy day's work before them, a motley but grave and decorous procession of apparently interminable length was seen coming over the hill on the side of which, "overlooking the little Mystic River, stood the large and, for its time, the imposing mansion of Mr. Gallup."

For a moment the master stood in blank dismay. The descendants of the friendly Mohegans and a remnant of their Pequod enemies, so nearly annihilated half a century before, were small in number when compared with their former strength, but they were still formidable as wedding-guests. They had heard that all the country-side had been invited to partake of Mr. Gallup's hospitality, and perhaps had imagined that such an invitation must include themselves. Such a conclusion would have been natural enough, "considering that he had always taken them, in a manner, under his protection, and they had always turned to him for advice and often for efficient help in time of need." Or it may have been that some practical joker had been at the pains to convey this impression, or, as

Mrs. Gallup's great-granddaughter opined, that " some slighted suitor had thought thus to cause annoyance to the bride." Whatever might have been the cause, the remnants of the tribes had come in all the security of invited and welcome guests — brave, squaw, and papoose.

With the prompt decision which characterizes most successful men, Mr. Gallup sprang upon the stone horse-block and proceeded to make an impromptu speech, " in the picturesque style in which he was an adept, and with which an Indian auditory was always pleased. He assured ' his children' that they were welcome, very welcome; but that they had mistaken the day for which they had been invited; that their day was the morrow, and that then he should set before them the best that could be had, a feast that should be worthy of them and of his friendship for them." In the slang of our own day, this contract was a large one, for the resources of the neighborhood had been already heavily drawn upon, and the line of the morrow's guests " as they wound their way back to their wigwams in open Indian file, as their native manner was, extended from the Gallup house well on to the head of the river, a mile or so away from it."

On the following day the dignified but hungry host came back again, " beplumed and blanketed in their best, and none went hungry or thirsty away."

For various good reasons, including the natural objections of a dainty housewife, this multitude was served out of doors, where immense iron kettles of clam and of fish chowders had been started to cook, over carefully tended fires, long before daylight.   In other kettles numbers of the wild ducks, which at that season had begun to be plentiful along the coast, were slowly stewing with onions. " Three young hogs, of about one hundred weight each, were roasted whole, also out of doors.   Hanging from the cranes in the great fire-places in the house were boiling big bags of Indian meal puddings, thickly studded with dried plums."   To be served with the puddings were pailfuls of a sauce made from West India molasses, butter, and vinegar.   Great baskets were filled with potatoes that had been roasted in the ashes, and other baskets were piled with well-baked loaves of rye and Indian bread.   All of these were dainties which the copper-hued guests could duly appreciate, especially with the addition of barrelfuls of hard cider and as much West Indian rum as it was deemed wise to set before them.

These particulars are all mentioned in the little diary from which I have culled so much, but, with the exception of the few things previously quoted, it says nothing about the viands that were served on the preceding days.   By this period the colonists had acquired the art of cooking to the best advantage most of the dishes which were peculiar to the country, and the wealthy among them had also a good many imported dainties.

No amusements in which women took part, save possibly as spectators, are mentioned, but we are told that the young men engaged in " rastling, quoits, running, leaping, archery and firing at a mark, but on the last day no muskets were allowed by reason of the Indians." Probably the women were all too much engaged in hospitable cares to indulge in any of the diversions considered suitable for them.

No wedding-journey followed the simple cere-mony. On the afternoon of the first day many of the invited guests — probably all of them on horse-back, save a few who may have followed on foot for a mile or so, for apparently there were no car-riages then in that region — escorted the newly wed-ded pair, the bride riding on a pillion behind her husband, to his house, the parsonage of the West Parish of Saybrook, Connecticut. Any further feasting might, even after a ride of twenty-five miles or more, have seemed superfluous, but a "valiant supper had been spread" by the care of Mr. Worthington's parishioners, wishing to extend a hearty welcome to his bride and the friends who had accompanied her, and all " were plentifully regaled with cold meats, roast and stewed oysters, cakes, comfits, chocolate and coffee."

" After the supper a hymn was sung by all, fol-lowed by a prayer and benediction. . . . After which," adds the young chronicler, "the friends all departed" (probably to the homes of Saybrook friends hospitably opened to receive them), "and my Grandfather and Grandmother, left alone together in their new Home, knelt down and prayed together for God's blessing."

CHAPTER XI

LIFE ON AN EARLY COLONIAL MANOR

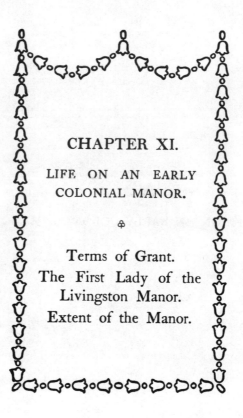

CHAPTER XI.

LIFE ON AN EARLY COLONIAL MANOR.

☙

Terms of Grant.
The First Lady of the
Livingston Manor.
Extent of the Manor.

THE holder of an American manor in colonial days, though of the highest social rank, was by no means an idle aristocrat living on an immense estate paying a proportionate revenue. In fact, if one of the wealthiest, he was also one of the busiest men of his generation. Both the conditions of the times and those upon which the manors were conferred made this a necessity. The manor granted to Robert Livingston in 1686 was almost, if not quite, as large as some of the German principalities of those days, and its possession implied a certain amount of extraneous wealth on the part of its owner to enable him to sustain his manorial authority with the fitting degree of power and prestige; but it was no sinecure.

Mr. Livingston's great domain, situated in what are now Columbia and Dutchess counties, New York, fronting for twelve miles along the Hudson River, and enlarging to the length of twenty miles on the Massachusetts border, thirty miles or so back from the river, was still, for the most part, a wilderness where Indians hunted the deer, or sometimes fired the hut and took the scalp of a too adventurous pioneer.

Robert Livingston was a far-seeing, politic man. As much as might be, he made friends of the wild tribes, paying them fairly for their lands, without regard to the fact that the royal grants were supposed to preclude any such necessity, and himself learning, and causing his sons to learn, the Indian tongues, that they might be delivered from the misunderstandings which were so frequent when the several parties to any agreement were dependent upon·the not always certain loyalty of the interpreters.

Nothing in North America was then so plentiful as land, and under the conditions imposed by the royal grants a poor man could not have afforded to accept a gift of the lordliest manor of them all. Within a specified time a certain number of families had to be brought from Europe and settled upon the granted territory, and their maintenance for the first few years assured. It is true that the settlers thus brought were expected to pay back at least a part of the first expenditure, but for the time the outlays were heavy, and comparatively few of the settlers made the losses good.

Farms were leased for long terms, usually for two lives and a half, a period which at that time was said to have averaged about fifty years.

In his novel of "Satanstoe," one of the most reliable of historical tales, Cooper says: "The first ten years no rent at all was to be paid; for the next ten the land [five hundred acres] was to pay sixpence currency per acre, the tenant having the right to cut timber at pleasure; for the remainder of the lease sixpence sterling was to be paid for the land and £40 currency or about $100 per year for the mill site. The mills to be taken by the landlord, at 'an appraisal made by men,' at the expiration of the lease; the tenant to pay taxes." The mill was evidently to be built by the tenant, "who had the privilege of using, for his dams, buildings, etc., all the materials that he could find on the land." To the landlords belonged the duty of constructing roads and bridges, and of making all improvements of a public nature. The rents were usually if not always paid in the produce of the land, which the manor's lord was obliged to get to market at his own expense in order to obtain the necessary cash for his varied undertakings. Such an arrangement would certainly seem to have been very liberal toward the tenant, and was doubtless so esteemed at the time, but in after years, when the descendants of the first tenants had forgotten the heavy advances which had been made by the ancestors of their landlords, and saw how easily the more recent settlers could make homes for themselves in the West, they considered themselves unjustly treated, and instituted the struggle for possession which is known to history as the "anti-rent war."

Of course, nothing of all this was foreseen at the beginning. The first manor lords undoubtedly thought that they were here founding immense holdings after the fashions of the motherland, and they proceeded in a thoroughly businesslike way to make all things secure for the prosperity of their heirs, who, when their time came, did not fail to appreciate what had been done for them.

Governor William Livingston of New Jersey, writing to his brother, the third lord of the Upper Manor, in 1775, remarked: "Without a large personal estate and their own uncommon industry and capacity for business, instead of making out of their extended tract of land a fortune for their descendants, our grand-parents and parents would have left us but a scant maintenance."

In this expression Governor Livingston seems to have included the manor ladies as well as their lords, and indeed it is plain that the very desirable "capacity for business" was equally needed by both, and the "hand of the diligent that maketh rich" is not an exclusively masculine possession.

The first lady of the manor of Livingston was Alida, the daughter of Philip Pieterse Schuyler, and widow of the Rev. Nicholas Van Rensselaer. Whatever dower in money or lands she may have brought to the aid of her astute second husband, she surely brought one still better in the sturdy

Dutch qualities of fidelity, thrift, and management. For warmth and strength of family affection, both Mr. and Mrs. Robert Livingston were long remembered among their descendants. Mrs. Livingston had come honestly by her executive and administrative ability. Her father had been a man of much influence in the colony, and her mother, *née* Van Slichtenhorst, survived her husband for twenty-eight years, so managing his large estate, over which she had full control, as to be reckoned the foremost woman in a colony which numbered many women of proved business ability.

The year of this marriage, 1683, was that in which young Robert Livingston made his first purchase of land from the Indians — a tract of two thousand acres. Two years later more land was added by purchase, and still one year later came the grant from the crown, when the whole was erected into a lordship or manor, conferring the "Court-Leet," "Court-Baron," and other rights and privileges which were for a long time more visible on the parchments than elsewhere.

On this estate of more than one hundred and sixty thousand acres,[1] on the banks of a small but for a short distance navigable tributary of the Hudson, was erected the first Livingston manor-house. Its last vestige disappeared more than a hundred

[1] Charles Carroll of Carrollton, writing in 1776, says that the Livingston Manor then comprised over 300,000 acres. This must have included almost 150,000 acres which had been gradually added by purchase to the original manorial grant.

years ago, when the present family residence, known as Oak Hill, was built, a mile or more from the ancient site.

Of the first house we only know that it was " thick walled, low browed and heavy raftered," after the then prevailing Dutch farm-house type, only much larger than was usual. We do not know that it was constructed in any way for defense, although it well might have been. Probably its builder trusted to keep the peace by his just and friendly dealings with the Indians, and he may also have been prepared for defense. He certainly had good reason to trust somewhat to the number of retainers gathered around him, a majority of whom, like all frontiersmen, would pretty surely be well armed against " big game," which would as surely include aggressively inclined Indians, if any there were; but this does not appear. From the rear of the broad-roofed dwelling stretched away the quarters of the slaves, the other outbuildings, and several barns, some of which were larger than the house itself.

There was much building of houses at various suitable points for the use of the tenant farmers and craftsmen brought from Great Britain, Holland, and Germany. To supply the timber for these dwellings sawmill machinery was imported and set up on the banks of the streams in the midst of the forests. Near these mills little settlements grew up with a celerity that was remarkable for the time, and spoke volumes for the executive and administrative ability of the manor's active lord. In a long, semi-detached wing of the manor-house carpenters and masons were fed and lodged during the long winters, while they did such preparatory work as might be possible to forward building operations in the various settlements in such moments as the weather would permit. With the adaptability of all true pioneers, these men could turn their hands to many things, and they manufactured in the manor's workshop and smithy many of the tools which otherwise must have been imported, as well as much of the rude furniture for the pioneer houses. Near by was the grist-mill which supplied flour and Indian meal to all the near settlements, as well as to many outside the manor for perhaps thirty miles up and down the river. On the home farm hundreds of swine and beef cattle were raised, slaughtered, and cured to supply scores of resident families and also for exportation. Here the wool of many hundreds of sheep was sheared, carded, spun into yarn, and woven into blankets and cloths to be used for the manor household and by those of the tenants not sufficiently " forehanded " to do this work for themselves.

In one room of the " great house " were held courts where all the difficulties common to frontier populations were adjusted, and in the same room were carried on the primitive banking operations of the newly opened region.

Near by were the docks, whence, when the

river was open, sloops were weekly departing, laden with salted meats, grains, peltries, and lumber, or returning with cargoes of all the countless things which could not yet be produced at home. Among these were many articles of luxury and rich household furnishings which must have seemed a trifle incongruous with their new surroundings.

Not far away stood the big "store," where all sorts of things, from wrought-iron nails to silks, and from "West Indian sweetmeats" to Dutch garden seeds, were sometimes sold for money, but oftener bartered for country produce and peltries, which would soon find their way to New York, and some ultimately to England, in ships owned by the enterprising Robert Livingston.

All these various branches of business implied the coming and going of many persons, and entailed an open-handed hospitality of the widest kind. For this the principal care and oversight fell upon the capable shoulders of Mrs. Livingston. It is traditionally related that the number of permanent dwellers which the manor-house roof sheltered during the first twenty years of the eighteenth century averaged something over thirty persons — this being exclusive of slaves, of whom there were more than a hundred having outside quarters, and of white employees. As strangers were always welcome, it was the custom to have beds of all sorts in a state of complete readiness for at least ten unexpected guests, while, at a pinch, a good many more could be accommodated without great inconvenience.

Among the dwellers in the manor-house was always the dominie, who, before the erection of the manor church in 1721, held services every winter Sunday in the great kitchen and adjoining dining-room, and in summer on the threshing-floor of the biggest barn. On each Sunday he preached one sermon in Dutch and another in English, and during the week he acted as tutor for Mr. Livingston's children and young relatives, as well as exercised a pastoral care over the members of his congregation. Other inmates were several more or less distant relatives of both Mr. and Mrs. Livingston, all of whom were probably expected to make themselves more or less useful in one way or another, for very few drones could have been tolerated in such an industrious hive.

Robert Livingston was a man of unusual cultivation for his time. It is said that he was a good classical scholar, and there is proof that he spoke and wrote the English, French, and Dutch languages with fluency and clearness. Both he and his wife had bright, quick, active minds, "were witty and wise," and both were possessed of much personal grace and charm, so that their house was regarded as a delightful home where all other attractions were added to the grace of hospitality.

The first manor of Livingston, with its many activities, its profuse hospitalities, and its strong contrasts, reminds one of Scott's descriptions of the rude baronial halls in the remote Scotch districts a few scores of years earlier than this. In the new land there was almost as much feudal authority over more diverse retainers, a greater display of costly plate, tapestries, and rich furniture, and the same lack of what were even then considered essential comforts for persons of like social position in regions less remote.

The wide hall and the long drawing-room of the big farm-house were wainscoted in panels. The mantels above the tile-bordered fireplaces were fancifully carved, and the walls were hung with costly Flemish tapestries; yet it is doubtful if, during the first three or four decades, any of the floors were carpeted, while that of the dining-room was certainly sanded, and a row of sheepskins, dressed with the wool on, was laid around the table in winter for foot-warmers. At the same time the table was laid with the finest naperies and much solid silver, interspersed with pewter and wooden dishes. During the earliest years there probably was not a single fork, and it is almost certain that there were few if any articles of china, and not many of earthenware. A dozen silver porringers bearing the original crest of the Livingstons, showing that they had been brought from Scotland by the first Robert, and a dozen goblets, or tumblers,

I am not sure which, bearing the same mark, were inherited as their share of the original plate, which was divided by weight, by two of my grandmother's brothers, who were descendants of the fifth generation, and who, it is grievous to know, had them melted to make handsomer but certainly less precious articles. As these persons were but two of the scores of Robert Livingston's descendants among whom his plate had been successively divided, some idea may be formed of its first amount.

The life led by Lady Alida Livingston in her wilderness manor-house was busy, bustling, dominant. Her household was kept well in hand, and so were her husband's business operations; not merely when he was present to guide them with his own masterful hands, but also during his long absence at his place in the colonial councils, or on his several journeys to England. Mrs. Livingston's family of six sons and daughters received every attainable advantage both in learning and accomplishments. Both she and her husband felt their responsibility as the founders of a family destined to honor and power. They gazed far into the future and builded wisely, yet they did not dream of a result to which their labors were tending.

Their descendants of the third and fourth generation, then grown to be a large, wealthy, keen-witted, and "clannish clan," were, with very few exceptions, found among the strongest opponents to

British power during the struggle of the colonies for independence, though well knowing that with their success would perish all dreams of the new-world baronies. The course of the three great manor families of Van Rensselaer, Van Cortlandt, and Livingston is alone a sufficient answer to the calumny that "great estates always made active Tories."

CHAPTER XII

PROSPEROUS DAYS ON A LATER MANOR

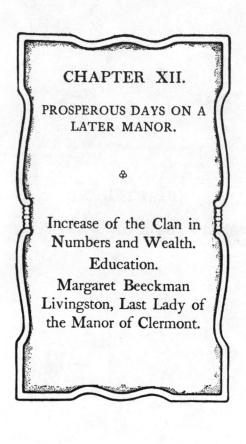

CHAPTER XII.

PROSPEROUS DAYS ON A LATER MANOR.

♣

Increase of the Clan in Numbers and Wealth.
Education.
Margaret Beeckman Livingston, Last Lady of the Manor of Clermont.

THE period from the founding of the first manor in the colony of New York to the beginning of the War of the Revolution was not quite a century, yet during the last third of that time home life on all the manors had greatly changed. What in the later time was held to be vast wealth had resulted from the wise plans and incessant labors of the founders, acting with the natural growth of the country. To such pleasant features as had existed in the earlier days many others had been added, while much of that which was unpleasant had disappeared. For miles along the eastern bank of the Hudson, above and below what is now Rhinebeck, almost every sightly eminence was capped with the fine residence of one of the grandchildren of the first lord and lady of the Livingston Manor. At all of these mansions cordial hospitality, abundant cheer, and all of what was then esteemed splendor, were to be found. There were at this time two Livingston manors, as a portion of the first (which was subsequently called the Upper Manor) had been set off to the founder's third son Robert as a reward for peculiarly important services. This segregated portion was indifferently called the " Lower Manor of Livingston " or " Clermont " until after the colonies had become States, when it became definitely known as Clermont, one of the most celebrated country-seats in America.

The manor ladies of the third generation and their successors of the fourth (though the title of these last had become one of courtesy only) were well-nigh queens on their own domains; but, like all queens who are not mere figureheads, they had many cares, which they accepted as frankly as they did the pleasures of their position.

Notions of political independence had for many years been growing through all the colonies, but of social equality there was scarcely a whisper. Certainly it was far from the thoughts of those who had belonged to good families in the old countries and had here been held in honor and had prospered to the extent of founding families of wealth. Perhaps no more frankly fervent aristocrats ever lived than the owners of the great colonial estates, whether these were situated on the banks of the James and the Chesapeake or on those of the Hudson. They were free from most of the restraints and traditions which often hung like fetters on the limbs of the kindred class in the motherland, and thus they were at liberty to enjoy their rank, wealth, and cultivation with an almost childish *naïveté.* Of this happy liberty they took the fullest advantage.

From the extreme limits of Van Rensselaer's manor on the north to that of the Van Cortlandts on the south, the eastern bank of the Hudson River from Albany to New York, and for a distance of from fifteen to thirty miles back from the river, was dotted by the handsome residences of as care-free, healthful, fine-looking, and happy a class as probably the society of any country has ever known. Its members were not driven by the fierce competition which embitters so many lives to-day, yet they had abundant and satisfying occupations. They had intermarried so freely that they seemed one great cousinry, all having a serene confidence in the invulnerability of their social position, which left them free to be jovial, hospitable, good-humored, and withal public-spirited to an unusual degree. The men had their offices, and their business hours in which to confer with their stewards and tenants, or with the men who conducted large enterprises of many sorts upon the strength of their capital and under their guidance. Into their capable and willing hands official positions naturally fell and were faithfully filled; but all these things were done in an atmosphere of large leisureliness, consequent upon the slow means of communication between distant points, which is almost beyond the conception of any in these electric days.

The men rode a great deal, or hunted after the

manner of their English cousins, or they made long expeditions into the unexplored regions of northern and western New York, partly, no doubt, with an eye to present profit or to future investments, but largely to gratify their innate love of adventure. Many of the sons were sent to the English universities of Cambridge or Oxford; but even if his college training had been received at King's (now Columbia) College, the education of no young man belonging to a wealthy and cultivated family was considered complete until he had made a tour of Europe, from one to three years being frequently consumed in this way.

Probably owing to the many dangers and the very serious discomforts which then beset an ocean voyage under the most favorable conditions, the sisters seldom accompanied their brothers, though there are a few known instances of daughters who went to England with their fathers, and there and in Scotland were most hospitably entertained by their more or less distant but ever "kindly kin." I have had the pleasure of reading some remarkably vivacious and charming letters from one such fortunate maiden, as they were copied by my relative, Mr. Livingston Rutherfurd, into his valuable but privately printed volume concerning the Rutherfurd family in America.

During the long absences of the male heads of the manor families the administration of their home affairs was left in the hands of capable stewards, who were always under the supervision of the manor ladies Margaret Beeckman, the wife of Judge Livingston, second (and last) lord of the Lower Manor, was the mother of Chancellor Livingston and of nine other goodly sons and daughters, most of whom eventually became distinguished persons. She displayed remarkable ability not only in fulfilling the duties of her high position during the lifetime of her husband, and in the management of his great estate after his decease, but also in the wise upbringing of her large family. An account-book kept in her own hand, with copious notes relating to crops and stock on her many farms, and to contracts with dealers in lumber, wools, and furs, as well as to the more intimate matters of household economy, shows a mind of much more than common business ability and breadth of view. The household supplies of every sort were on a scale commensurate with the family's social position, and would in themselves make most interesting reading for one who loves to make the past seem present by recalling the homely details of domestic life.

All the manor families had always encouraged what were then "home industries" in a strictly literal sense. But there were many things which the largest private expenditure could not produce in the new country, and Mrs. Livingston's old account-book shows that persons of wealth did not, for this reason, deprive themselves of much which they desired to possess. The things sent for from England, France, and Holland were varied, numerous, and costly. Great treasures of tapestries, pictures, inlaid cabinets, jewels, satins, velvets, and laces, as well as old wines, delicate porcelains, and expensive plate, must have been lost when the Clermont manor-house was burned by the British during our Revolutionary War. Among the imported articles were " An eboney Cabinet garnished out with Silver," which cost £40, and another of "Tortus Shell, garnished with Silver Guilte," costing £65 15s. " Two setts of bed curtayns broidered, lined & fringed," were £40 each. " Thirty six yards of Broussells carpett with border," £36. These prices probably covered freight charges as well as the original cost. All of these were great treasures for their day, and many such had been imported by Judge and Mrs. Livingston; but they exist no longer, save on the yellow but strong paper and in the good black ink of the leather-covered account-book kept for many years by Mrs. Margaret B. Livingston.

CHAPTER XIII

A COUNTRY PARSON'S WIFE

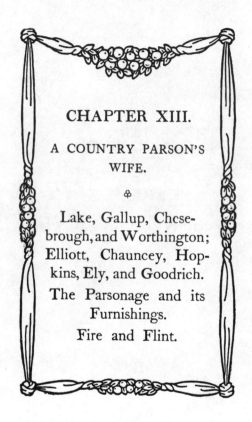

CHAPTER XIII.

A COUNTRY PARSON'S WIFE.

♣

Lake, Gallup, Chese-
brough, and Worthington;
Elliott, Chauncey, Hop-
kins, Ely, and Goodrich.
The Parsonage and its
Furnishings.
Fire and Flint.

THE roots of a strong character draw their nutriment from far beneath the surface; therefore it is less amiss than it might seem that we begin the simple story of this country pastor's wife by referring to that of another woman, who preceded her by more than a century.

During the twenty-five years which intervened between the landing at Plymouth and the battle of Naseby, New England had become the place of refuge for many of those to whom the mother-land had ceased to be home save in fond remembrance. Among these self-exiled were many who fled from the choice which they must make, if they remained in England, between their faith on the one hand and an inborn and inbred loyalty to their king on the other.

Of these was one Mrs. Margaret Lake, who is mentioned in our chapter on "A Pioneer Home." She was one of the original grantees of the township of New London, Connecticut, "sharing in all the grants and divisions of land made to the other settlers." Beyond this fact, and that she was a sis-

ter of the second Governor Winthrop's second
wife, little more than is told in that chapter is
known concerning her. The father of Mrs. Winthrop and Mrs. Lake belonged to that class which
has ever furnished the backbone of old England
— the frequently gentle born though often far
from wealthy class of hereditary landowners, living
at a distance from courts and fashions, but availing
themselves of the best educational advantages
afforded in their time. Many of this class fought
and died for the worthless Stuarts, and to it also
belonged the most upright and humane portion of
Cromwell's ever-valiant forces.

The years from 1645 onward to 1675, the date of
the battle with the Pequots known as the Great
Swamp Fight, were full of danger to the New
England colonists. Whatever their tender-hearted
descendants may think about the matter in these
days of security, there is no doubt that to our ancestors the Indian was a continual menace and terror, and no man gained more of the admiration of
his fellows than he who best held in check this
formidable foe. Among such defenders none in
what is now known as New London County, Connecticut, was held to be stronger of arm and more
dauntless of soul than Captain John Gallup, the
son of a father equally renowned in the same line.

The first Captain John Gallup was a grandson
of Thomas Gallup, owner of the manors of North
Bowood and Strode in Dorsetshire, England.

Being a younger son of a younger son, the emigrating Gallup may reasonably be supposed not to have possessed an unduly large share of this world's gear, but it is certain that he speedily became a man of some substance and much value in the colonies. His son, the second Captain Gallup, married Hannah, daughter of Mrs. Margaret Lake, thus bringing together the gentle and the warlike, and from their union sprang a race many of whose descendants have made their mark by council-fires and on the tented field, passing from one to the other as the needs of their country required, but flinching from no difficulty or danger when following what appeared to them to be their duty.

William Gallup, a son of the second John Gallup and Hannah Lake, married Sarah, a daughter of Samuel and granddaughter of William Chesebrough of Stonington, Connecticut. The last-named came from England in 1630 in Winthrop's fleet. Of Mr. Chesebrough it has been written that " he could frame a building or he could sit as judge in a case at law. He could forge a chain or draw up a plan for the organization of the municipal government. He could survey a tract of land or he could represent his town in the General Court and adjust its disturbed relations with the constituted [colonial] authorities." This shows him to have been a typical Yankee of the best sort — a man who could successfully turn his capable hands and brains to any useful thing.

It is said that Mr. William Chesebrough was a man of strong religious convictions, and certainly he must have enjoyed religious services, for it is recorded that in bad seasons, when the necessarily ill-made roads of the time were rendered more than usually impassable by heavy freshets and oozing frosts, he had been " known to start for church at a little after midnight in order to accomplish in good time the fifteen miles that lay between his home and the meeting house." It required both strength of muscle and conviction to render the best of men so zealous as that. But, with all his zeal, Mr. Chesebrough had a fund of humor which made his genial society sought by young and old until his death in 1667, while his "judicious mildness smoothed many public and private difficulties in the region where he was, in two senses, the first settler."

It is this Mr. Chesebrough's granddaughter, Temperance Gallup, whose marriage to the Rev. William Worthington is related in our account of " A Colonial Wedding," and it was one of the daughters of this couple who, in 1756 or 1757, became the wife of the Rev. Cotton Mather Smith of Sharon, Connecticut.

The Rev. William Worthington was the first settled pastor of the West Parish of Saybrook, Connecticut, where he died in 1756. Family traditions, coming down through several lines of descendants, unite in ascribing to him "great

blandness, urbanity and grace of manner combined with a keen and trenchant wit." He was
considered a learned man in his day, and as a
preacher "was distinguished for using the persua-
sions of the Gospel rather than the terrors of the
law." Mr. Worthington left five daughters and
one son — also William Worthington, a colonel
of patriotic troops during the Revolutionary War,
who died a bachelor. The youngest daughter
married Dr. Aaron Elliott, son of the Rev. Jared
Elliott of Killingworth, now Clinton, Connecticut.
Another married Colonel John Ely of Lyme, Connecticut, whose noble record of high patriotism is
but too little known. A third daughter married
Elnathan Chauncey. A fourth daughter married
Mr. William Hopkins. All of the sons-in-law of
the Rev. William Worthington were prominent
men in their several places of residence, and from
all of them have descended many persons of social
and intellectual distinction. It was the second
daughter, Temperance, who became the wife of the
Rev. Cotton Mather Smith of Sharon, Connecticut.

All of the sisters bore a contemporary reputation of being more accomplished than most of the
women of their time. Their father, being in advance of his age in considering that girls had as
much brain and as much use for it as boys, had
given to his daughters every attainable advantage.
Comparatively few of the pastors of Parson Worthington's generation paid visits to Europe, but

Mrs. Smith and one of her sisters in their girl-hood accompanied their father on a visit which he made to England. In the diary of Juliana Smith we find this "long and arduous" journey referred to several times, but with an exasperating brevity and incompleteness, as :

"When Mamma was with Grandfather Wor-thington in Boston, England, she heard a great Organ the tones of which rolled like the Ocean, and the whole soul melted to its music."

And again, writing in 1779 :

"When my Mother and Aunt were in England, thirty years ago, they were hospitably entertained at the country seats of some of my Grandfather's relatives there, and now we are told that one of them, who was an officer of the King's troops, and was an Ensign then, is now a Major, and is sick and a Prisoner in the hands of the Continentals. My Father will use every effort to have him brought to us, and then it is possible we may secure an ex-change for my Uncle Ely, who holds the same rank in our army, and is now a Prisoner in the hands of the British in New York."

This exchange, so much desired, was not effected, the doctor being found too useful as a physician among the sick prisoners confined in the "Old Sugar

House." It was nearly or quite at the close of the war when Dr. Ely, much broken in health, but not in spirit, was restored to his family.

Mr. S. G. Goodrich (Peter Parley), who was the grandson of Mrs. Chauncey, says that Mrs. Smith and her sisters were all "noted for their wide reading, their elegant manners, and their excellent house-wifery." The last two accomplishments may be taken without qualification, but in regard to the first claim it is necessary to make allowance for the conditions and times. Mr. Worthington's daughters certainly read Shakspere and Milton, for odd volumes of both of these classics still exist bearing the name of "Temperance Worthington, from her Father," written on fly-leaves. Both bear evidence of having been well read, though carefully used. (Books were far too costly and rare to be treated slightingly.) It is said that all of Mr. Worthington's daughters were good Latin scholars, and it is certain that at least one of them, Mrs. Smith, was a fairly good French scholar, speaking the language sufficiently well to act as interpreter when occasion required, as it sometimes did when the French troops were here during our Revolutionary War. The same useful office was filled by one of her sisters, Mrs. Ely, I think, at Newport, Rhode Island. Mrs. Smith taught the language of our allies to her own sons and daughters, giving them such an interest in it that at least two of them continued to read French and translate it with ease, even in their latest years. Where Mrs. Smith acquired her knowledge of the French tongue I do not know. It was a most unusual accomplishment in the New England of her time, and may have been gained in one of the Huguenot schools in New Rochelle. There is no proof that she attended one of these, but several circumstances seem to point that way; among them is the existence of some delicate specimens, made by "Madame Smith" and her daughters, of such needlework as was then universally known as "French embroidery."

The house to which Mrs. Smith came as a bride, in 1756 or 1757, was built a few years before that date by her husband's predecessor, the Rev. Mr. Searle. In spite of the fact that this dwelling was still in an admirable state of preservation, it was taken down in 1812 by my grandfather, who replaced it by a house of the then fashionable Grecian temple style of architecture.

The old house, as described to me, was large and heavily timbered, with its sides covered with overlapping cedar shingles. In front the hipped roof began to rise from a little above the ceiling of the first story, but sloped so little that the house was practically two stories high on that side. At the rear the roof slowly receded from the ridge-pole to the long stoep which ran from north to south across the back of the low-ceiled, many-windowed, wide and comfortable old manse. On the first floor four large rooms were grouped round the

central chimney, against which, and directly opposite to the outer door, was a square hall from
which a flight of stairs broken by a platform ran to
the second story. In accordance with the general
usage of the time, this outer door was divided into
upper and lower halves. It opened upon a stone
porch, provided with seats on the sides, and covered with an overhanging shingled roof unsup-
ported by pillars. At the time that my grandfather remembered it a portion of the stoep at the
rear had been inclosed to afford accommodations
for a summer kitchen, for washing clothes, and
a milk-room. At right angles with the house,
stretching eastward, there ran out from one corner
the immense woodshed, rendered necessary by the
incessantly devouring open fires; and near the eastern extremity of the shed were disposed the other
outbuildings. This was a great improvement upon
the common village usage of colonial days, which
was to cluster the woodshed and some of the
smaller outbuildings around the front door.

The village green, which is now so beautifully
elm-embowered, could then have been but a wide
and unkempt common, a pasture-ground where
scattered trees, the scant remains of ancient growths,
afforded shade to sheep, cows, calves, geese, and
sometimes even to swine.

Directly in front of the parsonage, shading its
porch, there stood an immense white-ash tree, believed to have been the largest of its kind in New

England, under whose giant branches the Wequag-
nock Indians had often built their council-fires.
This glorious tree lived and apparently flourished
until a great gale in August, 1893. My grandfather, William Mather Smith (who was born in
1786), said that within his recollection this tree
had never increased in apparent size. From the
front door to the gate, passing by and under the
great ash, was a short and irregularly flagged walk,
edged with box.

That one of the four principal rooms on the first
floor which opened by four large windows to the
west and south was occupied by the parson, both
as his study and as the class-room for his pupils.
There were then no theological seminaries, and
the young men who wished to be fitted for the
ministry studied with such pastors as were held in
the highest estimation for learning and ability.
About the time of the Revolutionary War the
Rev. Dr. Bellamy of Bethlehem, and the Rev. Cotton Mather Smith of Sharon, seem to have divided
between themselves the greater number of divinity
students of western Connecticut.

The parsonage furnishings would not strike the
modern eye as either abundant or very comfortable, yet there were comparatively few dwellings
of the day so well supplied. The dark mahogany
desk at which the Rev. C. M. Smith wrote hundreds of the sermons preached during his fifty-two
years' pastorate in Sharon is now in possession of

his great-great-grandson. Some of the fine old chairs and a sofa of the same unrivaled wood, the latter handsomely carved, but of severe outlines and unapproachable discomfort, are in the same ownership. An inlaid sideboard of mahogany and satinwood, which adorned the parsonage living-room, and which had belonged to the parson's father, is now owned by a great-great-granddaughter. These, with some small round mahogany stands for candles, an ebony-framed mirror, and a few other of the choice things which once stood in the parsonage, are all that now remain of its furnishings, save the portraits of King George III and Queen Charlotte. About these the only remarkable thing is that they exist at all, for they are on glass, and could not have survived save by dint of great care; and who could or would have bestowed this care immediately after the War of the Revolution? The parson and his wife were both very strong patriots, but it would seem that there might have lingered some feeling of personal loyalty to the old sovereigns, which, through it all, preserved their frail presentments with faithful care.

One of the comparatively few imported carpets at that time in the country lay on the parson's study floor. The living-room, across the hall from the study, and communicating with the kitchen behind it, had a carpet of heavy homespun woolen yarn, woven in a pattern of broad, lengthwise stripes. Such carpets had two merits: being as smooth of surface as the "Kensington art squares" of our day, they were much more easily swept than the ugly rag carpets; and being of wool, honestly spun and woven, were practically indestructible, save by moths. Some were still made in Connecticut well into this century. In the specimens which I have seen the colors were a rich red, a dark yellow, an indigo blue, a dingy purple, and a dusky green.

The bedroom of the parson and his wife, communicating directly with the study, and, through a passage, with the kitchen also, was a fireless room opening to the south. No wonder that in winter its tall four-poster was sheltered with heavily woven linen or wool curtains under the more decorative hangings of picture chintz. Bitterly cold and drafty, in zero weather, must have been the rooms whose only warmth was that which could escape from the adjacent rooms. No matter how generous might be the blaze of the open wood fire, far more of its heat made its way up the chimney-throat than to the opposite wall upon which its evening shadows gaily danced, and still smaller was the portion which could be coaxed into an adjoining room.

Heavy bed-hangings were a winter necessity before steam-heat, furnaces, or even stoves had been invented. My father and his brother, who well remembered these days, which, in country places, continued until about the end of their college terms in 1830 and 1832, have told me that on cold nights, after the fires had been covered, the wind often blew in great gusts down the wide-throated chimney, and that then the bed-curtains, heavy as they were, " blew like handkerchiefs in a gale," and they were glad enough of the additional protection for their ears and heads of warm nightcaps knitted by grandmother, mother, or cousin from the yarn even then still spun at home from the wool of their own sheep.

As friction matches did not come into general use until 1835 or thereabout, it was still the custom to bank the fireplaces with ashes at night until not an ember or spark of fire could be seen, just as similar fires had been banked for untold centuries before. If this precaution were not thoroughly taken the fires were an ever-imminent danger. On very cold and windy nights it was customary for some members of a family to take turns in sitting up to watch the fires.

My father, when a boy of eight or nine years, saw his father display to admiring neighbors " a wonderfully handy new invention by which fires could be readily kindled." Something like the trigger of a flint-lock musket was pulled, and a spark struck from the flint and steel, which ignited a bit of punk; this, being judiciously blown upon, set fire to splinters of resinous wood, and this, in turn, to carefully reared piles of splintered kindlings and well-seasoned logs. Before the advent of the "fire-sparker" of flint and steel, when the earliest riser of a family was so unfortunate as to find that the too slightly protected embers of the previous night's fires had burned themselves out, or that the too densely covered ones had been hopelessly smothered, it was his chilly task to wait and watch for the nearest chimney which should show rising smoke, and then to sally forth, with chafing-dish or foot-stove in hand, to "borrow coals."

CHAPTER XIV

HOME CARES IN A PARSONAGE

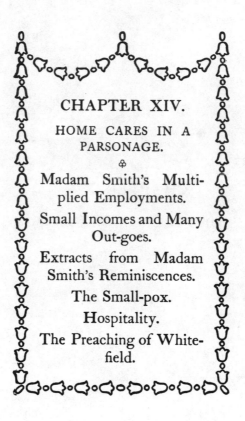

CHAPTER XIV.

HOME CARES IN A PARSONAGE.

✤

Madam Smith's Multiplied Employments.

Small Incomes and Many Out-goes.

Extracts from Madam Smith's Reminiscences.

The Small-pox.

Hospitality.

The Preaching of Whitefield.

ON Madam Smith's time, and for many a long year before and after, there was never a matron so wealthy that she had not her hands full of Martha-like cares. In general the richer the family the more arduous were these cares; but, of them all, not even the lady of a manor was so overburdened as was the parson's wife — the " madam," as she was generally styled, — so much was demanded of her, so multifarious were her duties. Ministerial stipends were then very small. Mr. Smith's salary at the time of his settlement, in 1754, was " 220 Spanish dollars or an equivalent in old tenor bills." In addition to this he was to receive, as what was then known as a " settlement," " 140 ounces of silver or an equivalent in old tenor bills, annually for three years." I believe that the yearly salary was subsequently increased, but do not know to what extent.

Salaries of four or even of three hundred dollars a year were considered liberal in country places until years after the Revolution. On such small sums, eked out by the produce from a certain number of acres of glebe-land, the minister was expected not only to support his own family, but to bear an undue share in the entertaining of strangers, as well as in aiding the neighboring poor. When, as sometimes happened, either the pastor or his wife had private property, still more was expected of them, and rarely indeed did they fail to respond to this expectation. Parson Smith, in a letter to his son-in-law, the Rev. Daniel Smith of Stamford, Connecticut, written in 1804, states that in his family there were maintained, in addition to his own six children, " an average of four penniless orphans during more than thirty years." These were not only fed and clothed, but educated, at the parson's sole expense. They, with his own children, the divinity students, and some of the boys whom he fitted for college and who resided with him, made a household of unusual numbers even for those days of large families, and entailed a great amount of care and labor on his own part, while his wife must have been very heavily burdened.

Long working hours were a necessity of the period. Five o'clock was the usual breakfast-hour in summer, and from six to half-past six in winter. Dinner was at noon, and tea at six in winter and seven in summer. This was so that the many tasks might be accomplished, for sufficient unto each day was its own work; it had no room for labors left over from the day before.

Wheat, rye, and corn were ground into flour and meal at the local mills, and salted fish, sugar, molasses, "West India Sweetmeats," and, excepting in war-times, tea, coffee, and chocolate, could be bought at the village stores; but aside from these, with long volumes of a country store's account-books, covering many years, open before me, I can hardly find a trace of any kind of provisions that did not have to be produced and prepared, from start to finish, by manual labor on the farms and in each individual household — and all this without the aid of any of the toil-saving devices which we now deem matters of course.

Perhaps an idea of some of these daily labors may be best conveyed by extracts from relations which were found among the old papers some years ago. Mrs. Smith in 1775 had made the week-long and perilous journey from Sharon, Connecticut, to Fort Ticonderoga, where her husband was dangerously ill of camp fever. All the way above Saratoga was through an unbroken wilderness. In after years Mrs. Smith told her story many times, and at least three of her children made notes of her narrations, from which the full story was compiled and told in the first person. Some years ago this was published, under the title of "Led by a Vision," in the "Home-Maker," a magazine then most ably edited by Mrs. E. P. Terhune — "Marion Harland." From this sketch the following extracts are taken:

"Your dear Father was among the very first to volunteer and received the honored post of Chaplain to the Fourth Connecticut Regiment, commanded by Colonel Hinman, and ordered to march to Ticonderoga. In common with many other well qualified Pastors my Husband had been in the habit of receiving into his family from time to time such young men as might wish, after leaving college, to fit themselves for the Gospel Ministry. At this time there were five such students in our house. My Husband provided for them by engaging his beloved friend, the Rev. Dr. Bellamy, of Bethlehem, to come and reside in our house, prosecute the education of the young theological students, supply the Sharon pulpit and attend to pastoral duties; a young friend of Dr. Bellamy engaging to perform like brotherly services for him in his parish. As Dr. Bellamy had two students of his own he brought them with him, which added to those already in our house made my family to consist of twenty-two persons besides servants.

"In our present state of peace and plenty [1795] this does not seem so very great a burden; but at that time when the exactions of the Mother Country had rendered it impossible for any but the wealthiest to import anything to eat or wear, and all had to be raised and manufactured at home, from bread stuffs, sugar and rum to the linen and woollen for our clothes and bedding, you may well imagine that my duties were not light, though I

can say for myself that I never complained even
in my inmost thoughts, for if I could even give up
for the honored cause of Liberty, the Husband
whom I loved so dearly that my constant fear was
lest I should sin to idolatry, it would assuredly
have ill become me to repine at any inconvenience
to myself. And besides, to tell the truth, I had no
leisure for murmuring. I rose with the sun and
all through the long day I had no time for aught
but my work. So much did it press upon me
that I could scarcely divert my thoughts from its
demands even during the family prayers, which
thing both amazed and displeased me, for during
that hour, at least, I should have been sending all
my thoughts to Heaven for the safety of my beloved Husband and the salvation of our hapless
Country; instead of which I was often wondering
whether Polly had remembered to set the sponge
for the bread, or to put water on the leach tub, or
to turn the cloth in the dying vat, or whether wool
had been carded for Betsey to start her spinning
wheel in the morning, or Billy had chopped light-
wood enough for the kindling, or dry hard wood
enough to heat the big oven, or whether some
other thing had not been forgotten of the thousand
that must be done without fail or else there would
be a disagreeable hitch in the house-keeping; so
you may be sure that when I went to bed at night,
I went to sleep and not to lie awake imagining all
sorts of disasters that might happen. There was

generally enough that had happened to keep my mind at work if I stayed awake, but that I very seldom did. A perfectly healthy woman has good powers of sleep. . . .

"On the third Sabbath in September Dr. Bellamy gave us a sound and clear sermon in which God's watchful Providence over his People was most beautifully depicted and drew tears from the eyes of those who were unused to weeping, and during the prayer-meeting in the evening the same thought was dwelt upon in a way showing that all who spoke and prayed felt that our God is indeed a Father to all who trust him; so that on that night I went to bed in a calmer and more contented frame of mind than usual. I had, to be sure, been much displeased to find that our supply of bread (through some wasteful mismanagement of Polly's) had grown so small that the baking would have to be done on Monday morning, which is not good house-keeping; for the washing should always be done on Monday and the bakings on Tuesday, Thursday and Saturday. But I had caused Polly to set a large sponge and made Billy provide plenty of firing so that by getting up betimes in the morning we could have the brick oven heated and the baking out of the way by the time Billy and Jack should have gotten the clothes pounded out ready for boiling, so that the two things should not interfere with each other. The last thought on my mind after committing my

dear Husband and Country into our Maker's care
for the night, was to charge my mind to rise even
before daylight that I might be able to execute
my plans. . . .

"As early as three o'clock in the morning I
called Nancy and Judy, Jack and young Billy,
but would not allow old Billy to be disturbed;
whereat the rest marvelled, seeing that I was not
used to be more tender of him than of any of the
other servants, but rather the less so in that he was
my own slave that my Father had given to me
upon my marriage. But I let them marvel, for
truly it was no concern of theirs, and by five
o'clock 'the bread was ready to be moulded, the
hickory coals were lying in a great glowing mass
on the oven bottom, casting a brilliant light over
its vaulted top and sending such a heat into my
face when I passed by the oven mouth that it
caused me to think then, as it always does, of
Nebuchadnezzar's fiery furnace, seven times heated.
Young Billy was already pounding out the clothes
and over the fire Jack was hanging the great brass
kettles for the wash, while Nancy and Judy had
made ready the smoking hot piles of Johnny cake,
the boiler of wheat coffee (which was all we could
get in those days, and a poor substitute it was for
good Mocha) and the big platter of ham and eggs
and plenty of good potatoes roasted in the ashes,
which is the best way that potatoes can be cooked,
in my opinion."

The diverse housewifely cares indicated in the foregoing extracts show but a few of the many which fell to the lot of all colonial women of the better classes. Upon the minister's wife devolved still other duties. She was expected to assist at all the births, weddings, and funerals, not only in the French sense, but as an active helper. It is related of Madam Smith that for thirty years it was into her hands that most of the new-born babies of her husband's parish were committed for their first robings. And there being then, in country places at least, no undertakers, as we now understand the term, but in their stead only cabinet-makers who made coffins as well as cradles, chairs, and tables, Mrs. Smith shared with other ladies the last sad offices for friends and neighbors.

In times of general sickness — which were much more frequent than now, owing to the ignorance of sanitary precautions and all means for controlling contagious disease — both the pastor and his wife were ever at the service of the flock. It is recorded in Sedgwick's valuable history of Sharon that in the winter of 1784–85 there was "a three months' visitation of the town by the small-pox, during which seven hundred persons out of a population of about two thousand had the dreaded disease, either naturally or by inoculation," and that throughout this time of distress Parson Smith and his wife "spent their entire time in close attendance upon the sick and dying."

The entertainment of strangers was a duty which perhaps devolved more frequently upon the family of a country pastor than it should have been permitted to do, but there were occasions when the hosts felt themselves much more than repaid.

Such an occasion came to Parson and Mrs. Smith in the month of June in 1770. On the 18th of this month came the Rev. George Whitefield on his last and greatest preaching tour. He had passed up the Hudson River, stopping to preach at all towns which would give him a hearing, including Albany, whence he passed onward to Schenectady. Turning at this point, he had come southward again, visiting townships from twenty to thirty or more miles back from the eastern bank of the river, and preaching wherever allowed to do so in the churches, otherwise in the open air, until he reached Sharon. Here, as had happened in many other places, "there was," says Mr. Sedgwick, "considerable opposition to his being permitted to preach in the meeting-house," but Parson Smith's influence, always inclined to the liberal side on any question, prevailed, and the church doors were opened, and, "that all the hearers from this and the neighboring towns might be well accommodated with seats, extensive scaffolds were erected all around the house."

A few of the children and many of the grandchildren of those who had heard Whitefield in Sharon on this occasion were living in my girlhood, and marvelous indeed must have been the eloquence that was followed by such deep and far-reaching results, and was remembered so long.

Most marvelous must the preacher's successful efforts have seemed to one who, like Madam Smith, had spent the entire previous night by his bedside, burning dried stramonium-leaves that he might inhale the smoke, and in various other ways doing her utmost to enable the sufferer to get his breath, under the violent attacks of asthma which, three months later, ended his career.

Mrs. Smith and others had feared, all through this anxious night, that their revered patient would pass from earth before the morning's sun should rise, yet as it rose his sufferings became gradually less. He had two or three hours of refreshing sleep, followed by draughts of strong coffee, and before the noon came he was able to preach such a sermon as even he could seldom do, while his grand voice, " as soft as a flute and as piercing as a fife," carried for almost incredible distances, not only his text, " Marvel not that I said unto thee, Ye must be born again," but all save the finer shadings of his message.

The letter of thanks and farewell sent by Mr. Whitefield from his dying bed at Newburyport, Massachusetts, did not reach Parson and Mrs. Smith until more than a month after its writer had there drawn his last agonized breath; but it was long cherished as a token from an angel visitant.

CHAPTER XV

SUNDAYS AND OTHER DAYS IN THE PARSONAGE

CHAPTER XV.

SUNDAYS AND OTHER DAYS IN THE PAR-SONAGE.

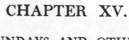

From Sunset to Sunset.
The Weekly Ablution.
Care of the Teeth.
Long Services.
Catechizing.
Sunday Night.
Fashions and Clothes.
An Evening of Sacrifice.

ROM the beginning of the New-Englander's Sabbath, at sunset on Saturday evening, the housewife must have found that portion of sacred time anything but a period of rest. The Saturday evening meal must be hastened, that the dishes might be washed in secular time. Personal ablutions were held to be labor not unbefitting the holy day, and from the earliest times in the New England colonies, the Saturday evenings were devoted, first to an hour's catechizing, and then to the conscientious scrubbing (this word sounds a little harsh, but it is probably the correct one to describe the process) of each person in the family, beginning with the youngest and concluding with the oldest members of the household.

As special rooms for bathing, with hot and cold water to be had with the turning of the faucet, were then undreamed-of luxuries, some have supposed that in the frequently excessive cold, and under the lack of all conveniences, our ancestors were neglectful of the grace of personal cleanliness. This is, in all probability, a grave mistake. Both tradition and written contemporary evidence go to prove that personal cleanliness was enjoined as a religious duty, and that it was a duty religiously fulfilled, under whatever difficulties.

Hot water could only be procured by heating in great iron pots over the open fires, and the tubs employed for bathing were in general the same which were used for the clothes-washings on Mondays, but not always. Some tubs were made for bathing purposes only, of cedar, and large enough for a tall man to lie in at full length. When the mother of the Rev. C. M. Smith came to Sharon from Suffield, Connecticut, about 1770, she brought with her a tub of this sort. As there were no stated rooms for bathing, the tubs were usually left in the cellars through the week, that they might not become dry enough to leak. If a fire were not kept in the best room all the rest of the week, one would be lighted there on every Saturday during the cold season, and maintained until late on Sunday night. This left free the fires in the kitchens for the servants, and those in the living-rooms for the family. Here the carpets, if any, were protected, and the tubs were set, each one shielded from view on all sides, save that nearest the fire, by heavy woolen coverlets or blankets hung over clothes-horses. With the generous size of the fireplaces of those days, as many as three or even more such curtained cabinets might be made in front of each fire. As much cold water as was desired was poured into each tub and was then brought to the required temperature by the addition of boiling water from the great iron or brass kettles.

The carrying out the water that had been used by each bather, and emptying the tubs at a little distance from the house, occasionally into a sub-surface drain, as at the parsonage, or, as in most cases, into shallow ditches, and of refilling the tubs, was severe labor, and would probably devolve upon the strongest of the servants or members of the family.

Certainly much, and probably all, of the soap used in the colonies was of home manufacture, and was so harsh in its quality that as little of it as possible was used upon the person. Those who were careful for their complexions rarely used any soap about their faces, but instead softened the water by a very little lye made from the ashes of hard woods. Rose-water of home distillation and various unguents were then applied to heal the smart. In warm weather buttermilk was considered excellent for the complexion, and in severe winter weather cider brandy was used by some, and an ointment of mutton tallow and lard by others.

The house-mistress had not only to see that all was in readiness for this great weekly ablution, but that none for whom she was responsible should escape it. Nothing but a case of severe illness was allowed to excuse any inmate of a self-respecting household. This state of things lasted until within my mother's remembrance. She was born in 1810, and one of her earliest recollections was of seeing old "Kongo Sally," armed with a stout switch, driving the young darkies, some of whom were her own grandchildren, in from the outbuildings in which they sought refuge, to undergo their weekly scrubbing from her merciless hands and those of one or two assistants.

As dentistry was an art still in the future, decayed teeth were the rule rather than the exception among adults until well into the present century; yet persons of refined instincts never omitted cleansing the teeth. Juliana Smith, writing to her brother in 1782, says: "Peggy Evertson has showed me a present her father brought her from Albany. It is a brush for the teeth made of fine, stiff, white bristles set in a back of mother of pearl. It is better than the sassafras twigs which Tite Cæsar fringes out for us, because with the brush you can better cleanse the backs of the teeth. You wanted to know what you should bring me from New Haven when you come back, so I write about this, if so be you might find me one. Only it need not have so fine a back, one of wood or horn would please me as well." Tooth-brushes are mentioned in the Verney papers, about 1650, as "elegant trifles now used by the ladies of the French Capital." But smoothly rounded bits of wood, sharpened at one end, and at the other finely splintered and then pounded into the semblance of a round paint-brush, were in use in England long before that, and washes for " cleanseing the teeth and sweetning the breath " are mentioned in the outfit of the child-bride of Richard II.

The Sharon parsonage was distinguished above many others of its time in that the best of water for all purposes was brought into the house from a distant spring by a primitive aqueduct of cedar logs, bored through their length to form tubes, then tightly fitted together, and laid at a depth of several feet beneath the surface to protect them from the frost, while the refuse water was discharged in a similar way in the opposite direction at a distance from any dwelling. Within a few years some of these logs have been dug up, still in a state of fair preservation, while the decaying remains of others lay near by. From the same spring which supplied the parsonage the delicious water was similarly conducted into the stone mansion of Dr. Simeon Smith. There still remains the basin which once received and discharged the water in this house. It is of smooth and finely grained limestone, about fourteen inches in diameter at the top, and of equal depth. Since the introduction of modern plumbing this basin has been used as a pot to hold growing plants out of doors.

Of course the Puritan parson's wife was expected to attend every Sabbath service as strictly as himself, and perhaps it was not always either pleasant or convenient for her to do so; but it is not necessary to dwell upon that part. Quite enough has been said by the last generation or two of persons who, judging others by themselves, fancy that two long sermons and a prayer-meeting must have wearied both the souls and the bodies of our ancestors, as they would our own. This is not at all probable. They really liked the long preachments, the endless prayers, the unmusical singing. Nay, more, they loved all of them. They saw and heard with spiritual eyes and ears, with an inner uplifting which imparted light, perfume, and harmony to their barren surroundings. I do not say that there were not many who inwardly and some who openly rebelled at these things, but they were in a minority. There is every proof that the majority really enjoyed what we should now consider as very tiresome Sundays.

To walk, to ride on horseback, or to drive in springless wagons over miles of often intolerable roads, and then spend two hours in a fireless church on a winter day, and, after an hour's interval, to spend another two hours in the same way, does not seem very inviting to us; but, in addition to the strong religious motives to sustain them, these people had social motives as well. The Sunday services were pleasures all the more valuable because they were shared in common. The noon intermission was a season of social communion most keenly enjoyed, and the still later adjournment of all to the

catechizing at the parsonage was made interesting
by the permitted freedom of discussion, and the
subsequent interchange of views and friendly greetings. Books were scarce; newspapers, in our
sense, were non-existent; and of such periodicals as
there were, but few would be taken in a small
township. Any new books or papers would first
find their way to the parson, and every intelligent
stranger passing through the place would call at
the parsonage, paying for his entertainment by
bringing as much news from the outside world as
he had been able to collect on his journey, and receiving as much local information as he could get
to carry away with him and distribute as he proceeded on his travels. The parsonage was an intelligence exchange, and the parson was expected
to give from the pulpit any new religious or political information that he had gained through the
week, and, after the Sunday afternoon catechizing,
his family shared with him the pleasure and duty
of imparting any bits of more personal interest that
had come to their knowledge.

It was fortunate for the madam that Puritan
usage required that as little cooking as might be
should be done on the Sabbath, for otherwise time
and strength would both have failed her; but the
sacred hours ended with the setting of the sun,
and after this there was cooked and served the best
meal of the week, which was made an occasion of
real festivity, and enjoyed with the keen zest im-

parted by long anticipation, by the easy assurance that it had been well earned, and by the certainty that, though the morrow's toils were lying in wait, they could not spoil the pleasures of this hour.

During this privileged time after the "Sunday night supper," the young folks separated into groups, unrebuked by their elders. The children played games, elderly men talked of theological dogmas, politics, and crops, and women of their household employments and clothes.

Fashions, like materials, were then much more durable than now. As there were no fashion-papers, intelligence on this subject could only be transmitted from mouth to mouth. A new paper or cloth pattern was a treasure indeed. It must not be supposed that these notable women talked only about their own clothes, and exchanged only the patterns of women's and infants' apparel. The attire of husbands and brothers was a matter of equally practical concern to them. The parson's preaching-suit — black cloth knee-breeches and straight-cut coat — might be made by some itinerant tailor, passing from house to house during the winter, as was the custom of the day, or might in a few instances have been bought in distant New York or New Haven; and the sheer linen for his bands was probably imported from Holland: but all his other garments (and those of most of the men in his parish), including the long, knitted silk stockings (worn over woolen ones in winter), were necessarily of home manufacture. Besides the linen for the minister's bands, the silk for his stockings was imported; but every thread of the rest of his apparel, from the finest linen for his handkerchiefs and shirts, to the woolen yarn for his underclothes, was grown or raised upon his own ground, tilled and cared for, harvested and cured if it were flax, or sheared and carded if it were wool, by his own hands or those of his employees, at least some of whom must have been slaves; and their clothing also had to be provided for by his labor and foresight.

All New England ministers were to a certain extent farmers as well as pastors, and where the parson's labors ceased those of the madam and her daughters and women began. Men hatcheled the flax, and both men and women carded wool. The spinning was always the work of women, while weaving was done principally by men. Between them they spun, knitted, wove, fulled and dyed, cut, fitted, and adorned all the textile fabrics worn. Carpets were seldom woven at home, and damask table-linen, if not imported, was usually the work of a professional weaver. So, too, were the blue-and-white or green-and-white all wool or cotton-and-wool coverlets of elaborate patterns of which so many still remain; but the yarn or thread for them all, whether linen, cotton, or wool, was spun at home. Sheets, blankets, and all simply striped or checked table-linen and bed-hangings were woven as well as spun at home.

The summers were especially busy, neither men nor women, bond nor free, those in the prime of life nor the aged, nor children, could idle away the long summer days. The great grain-fields of the West were still unawakened from their ages of slumber. Wheat, rye, buckwheat, corn, oats, must all be raised here.

With agricultural implements so imperfect that no modern farmer would condescend to use them, the labors of planting, sowing, haying, and harvesting were great. In these days we know the evils of competition and the nervous strain from the perpetual unrest of our lives, but we know neither the disadvantages of severe manual labor nor much about the ceaseless toil necessary in summer to provide for winter's daily physical needs. These labors were healthful in their nature, but pitiless in their exactions.

Winter's toils were sufficiently arduous. Providing the fuel for the indispensable and endlessly craving open wood fires was alone a heavy task, and there were many others, such as the daily care of the horses, sheep, swine, and fowls; yet in winter it was possible to find time to read, write, and study, as well as to enjoy such social gatherings as might combine amusement with work. What some of these pleasures were may be seen in other chapters. Here we will only glance at one which was peculiar to the Revolutionary period.

Bullets had become very scarce. Madam Smith, like most well-to-do matrons of her time, possessed a goodly store of pewter plates, platters, cups, bowls, and porringers. Several of the neighboring ladies were equally well supplied. On a certain early spring evening in 1777 Madam Smith invited all to come and bring with them every pewter dish which they could spare. Before the time for separation came many gallons of good bullets had been made from the cherished pewter articles, which had been melted and merrily run through bullet molds, and a good supper had been heartily enjoyed. For many evenings after this one of cheerful sacrifice, there were held from house to house so-called " trencher bees," whereat the young men cut and shaped maple and poplar wood into dishes, which the women made smooth by scraping with broken glass, and polished with the clean white sand of powdered limestone. Madam Smith, and probably most of the other contributors to the bullet fund, possessed a good deal of pretty Lowestoft and Delft, as well as Canton blue china, but the every-day use of such fragile dishes was not to be thought of, especially in war-time, when they could in nowise be replaced; hence the necessity for the return to the primitive wooden dishes of the seventeenth century.

All existing records of Madam Smith — and they are many — prove her to have been one of those noble women, a few of whom are to be found in all countries and in every age, who are so cheerfully brave that they face suffering and danger in all forms, unconscious that they are doing anything more than any other would do, yet so lovable and so gracious in their strength that they are mourned until the last one who knew them has himself passed from earthly scenes. Madam Smith died in 1800, and for all the years after her decease until her husband and the latest lingerer of her children had departed to join her, the letters which passed between the survivors are filled with touching references to the beloved wife and revered mother.

CHAPTER XVI

MANOR LADIES AS REFUGEES

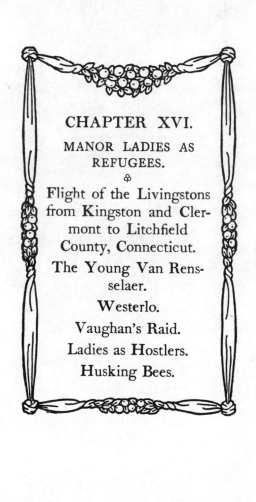

CHAPTER XVI.

MANOR LADIES AS REFUGEES.

⚜

Flight of the Livingstons from Kingston and Clermont to Litchfield County, Connecticut.

The Young Van Rensselaer.

Westerlo.

Vaughan's Raid.

Ladies as Hostlers.

Husking Bees.

DURING the War of the Revolution those manors which were situated on or near the Hudson River were exposed to the ravages of both parties in the struggle — some from the British forces and some from the Continental armies, according to the side which had been espoused by the respective owners of the manors. The De Lanceys were not technically manor-holders, but their estates were so large that they were popularly reckoned as such, and they, with the family from the Phillipse Patent, sought refuge within the British lines, while the patriotic Van Rensselaers, Van Cortlandts, and Livingstons retired to regions that were so far from the harassed territory as to promise comparative safety.

First, the Van Cortlandts fled from the Neutral Ground, carrying as many of their household possessions as they could by sloops, and having their flocks and herds driven up through the country in patriarchal fashion, to seek refuge among Mrs. Van Cortlandt's relatives, the Livingstons, in Columbia and Dutchess counties. But by the autumn of 1777 this neighborhood had become almost as full of danger as the lower counties, and all prominent persons, both refugees and natives, were obliged to strike their tents and seek shelter in happier regions.

For many of them the new haven of refuge existed in the northwestern corner of the State of Connecticut, about midway between the Hudson and Connecticut rivers, and from eighty to one hundred miles from salt water. Here, at a safe distance from water-highways, in one of the healthfulest and most placidly beautiful of highlands, the horrors of war never penetrated, though its terrors were abundantly known to those — and they were a majority of the inhabitants — who had sent their best beloved to battle for the cause which they held dearer than life or estates.

The earliest of the manor families to take advantage of this haven of rest among the hills appears to have been that of Mrs. Van Rensselaer, widow of the sixth patroon, and mother of the delicate boy who afterward became the honored General Van Rensselaer, and who, even after the new state of things had relegated such titles to the realm of the past, was by courtesy styled the seventh patroon. The lad's mother was a daughter of Philip Livingston, a signer of the Declaration of Independence, and upon this grandfather the general care of the promising boy's education devolved until Mr. Livingston's death in June of 1778. Singularly enough, there appears to be no published reference to the sojourn of young Van Rensselaer in Connecticut, it being stated that he went directly from Kingston, New York, to Harvard College. Yet the proof is positive that during the summer of 1777 the young patroon and his mother, who had first retired to Philip Livingston's temporary residence at Kingston, finding the dangers to which the young heir was there exposed, retreated to Connecticut in the safer recesses of the Litchfield County hills. Here they continued to reside during much, if not all, of the following year. Probably they were led to the beautiful village of Sharon by the previous friendship of Mrs. Van Rensselaer with the wife of the Rev. Cotton Mather Smith, who was pastor there. When the first of these ladies was Catherine Livingston of New York city, and the second was Temperance Worthington of Saybrook, Connecticut, the two had somewhere become intimate friends — possibly at school in New Rochelle, where there were at that time several rather noted private schools conducted by the refugee Huguenots or their immediate descendants.

Sometime during 1775 the widowed Mrs. Van Rensselaer had married her second husband, the Rev. Eilardus Westerlo of the Reformed Dutch Church. In the papers at my command she is never called Mrs. Westerlo, but, probably from habit, is indifferently referred to as "Mrs. Van R." or as the "Mother of the young Patroon" or as "Catherine Livingston," though there is little doubt that Mr. Westerlo was of the party, for I find that one of that name occupied Mr. Smith's pulpit twice in November of 1777; but I find no other mention of him, while it is recorded that "young Van R. and his mother," and a little later the Rev. John Rodgers of the Brick Church of New York city, were received into the family of the Rev. C. M. Smith, under whose direction young Stephen Van Rensselaer and the "Parson's son," afterward Governor John Cotton Smith of Connecticut, prosecuted their studies for college as diligently as if such a thing as war was never heard of. The first intention of young Van Rensselaer's guardians had been that he should enter Yale College, of which his grandfather and the latter's four brothers had been graduates, but eventually Harvard was chosen as being safer from the raids of the enemy.

The arrival of this little company in advance of the main body of the refugees is traditionally said to have been due to repeated attempts on the part of armed bands of Tories to abduct the wealthy young patroon in the hope of extorting a heavy ransom. The later flight of the family of Philip Livingston and the other families that had been sheltered under his roof at Kingston was extremely hurried, but probably not quite unpremeditated; otherwise there could not have been so much household furniture and stuff brought across the river and over the forty or more miles of intervening hills and dales.

On the day of the departure from Kingston a "mounted runner" had been sent ahead to secure in Sharon such accommodations as might be available. The women and children were therefore immediately provided with shelter, but for several nights their male companions were obliged to sleep in haymows. Refugees from places farther down the Hudson River had been for days, and even weeks, straggling into the little village, and many of them were without money or goods, so that the resources of the hospitable inhabitants had been already severely taxed.

Next door to the parsonage, where the first of the manor parties had been received, was a handsome but not very large brick cottage, owned by Robert G. Livingston, which, during this season of fear, must have been more than sufficiently filled. Mr. Robert G. Livingston's family was numerous enough to crowd it without counting servants, and to this number was now added the family of his relative Philip Livingston, and that of the latter's daughter Sarah and her husband, the Rev. John Henry Livingston. The house — which, by successive additions, all of them fortunately in keeping with the architecture of the original structure, is now a truly beautiful as well as spacious cottage belonging to the Rev. C. C. Tiffany — then contained but three rooms on the ground floor and three on the second, with two tolerably spacious attics over all; and, like the five loaves and two small fishes, what were they among so many? The united families probably did not consist of less than twenty persons, exclusive of slaves. It is true that "the boys" seem to have found lodgings in neighboring houses, though all were already crowded with the patriot refugees from the Neutral Ground and the upper river counties — refugees of every age and rank, and in great numbers. Probably this quiet little village will never again be so densely populated as it was during the eventful months of the last third of the year of Burgoyne's surrender.

In September of that year all things were looking dark enough for the patriot cause. Burgoyne and his dreaded Indian allies were threatening from the north. Sir Henry Clinton, working up toward Burgoyne from New York, had intended to form a juncture with him. Sir Henry had sent up the Hudson a band of one thousand men under General Vaughan — a name long afterward held in abhorrence from New York to Albany. This band did some gallant fighting in the capture of Forts Montgomery and Clinton, and some good work for their side in removing the chains and booms which General Putnam had caused to be stretched across the river to impede navigation; but beyond these things it "accomplished nothing save a good deal of safe and cautious marauding."

This included the burning, pillaging, and in far too many cases the murder of the defenseless.

In those days war was never undertaken as a philanthropic enterprise, and that boats and other means of transportation, as well as mills and stores of all sorts, should be destroyed was to be expected : but when village after village, however small, strategically unimportant, or utterly incapable of resistance each might be, was given up to relentless pillage and then burned, great was the crop of bitter feelings sown, to be reaped by the loyalists when the fortunes of war eventually turned against them, especially as it was well known that to many a retired farm-house sheltering only women and children, as well as to more pretentious but still equally unprotected residences, the torch had been applied by the hands of neighboring Tories who once had been friendly to their owners. After the war, whenever there was found to exist the bitter spirit which cast the loyalists forth by thousands to take an unwilling refuge in the wilds of Nova Scotia and New Brunswick, it was discovered, upon investigation, that acts of gratuitous cruelty had many times been committed by them, or at least by those whose cause they had espoused, for in this case, as in all others, the innocent suffered with the guilty.

On the Manor of Clermont, or the Livingston Lower Manor, as it was indifferently called, near Rhinebeck and Red Hook, on the eastern bank of

the Hudson, stood the fine residences of the widow
of Judge Robert R. Livingston and of her son,
Robert R., afterward known as the first and very
able Chancellor Livingston of the State of New
York. Both of these mansions had long been
marked for destruction, and their inmates had received repeated warnings to that effect, even before
the general raid of Vaughan's troops had advanced
from the Neutral Ground in the early October of
1777; yet the families had not left their homes
until sure that the enemy was within a few hours'
distance.

At this very time two British officers, a wounded
Captain Montgomery and his surgeon, prisoners on
parole, were being most hospitably entertained and
cared for in the family of the elder Mrs. Livingston. Tradition holds that this Captain Montgomery was a relative of Mrs. Livingston's late
son-in-law, General Montgomery, who at an early
period of the war had fallen while leading the Con-
gressional troops to the assault of Quebec. However this might be, both of the British officers
begged their hostess not to forsake her home,
promising that their presence should be a sure protection to all under the roof that had so kindly
sheltered them. It is stated that Mrs. Livingston
refused to take advantage of the offer on the
ground that she could not accept any favors shown
to herself unless the same should be extended to
her neighbors. But it may also have been that

she did not have sufficient confidence in the power of her two friends to accomplish all that their hearts prompted. It would certainly seem that even if the owners of the house did not choose to remain and run the risk of personal violence, the presence in it of the invalid British officer and his physician might have protected the dwelling from fire and pillage. As this did not prove to be the case, the supposition is that their intercessions were of no avail.

Mrs. Livingston's flight was barely in time. The news of the pillagings lower down the river was not confirmed soon enough to enable the fugitives to make many preparations. Wagons which for some weeks had been held in readiness for any such emergency were hastily laden with pictures, silver, and other of the most precious possessions, and with the most necessary articles of furniture, clothing, and bedding. Of the rest, as much as possible was hidden in a deep ravine but a short distance from the rear of the house, underneath trees which had been felled across it some months before. Above the furniture in the cave thus formed was scattered a thick covering of hay. The entrance was on the lower end of the ravine and escaped the notice of the marauders. The books forming the fine library of the late Judge Livingston were laid in the dry basin of a large fountain in the front of the house, which had been allowed to get dry from the difficulty and expense attending repairs at this time. In this basin the books were covered first with old sloop sails, and then with barn-yard refuse. A number of these volumes were afterward found in fairly good condition, and some are still preserved in the families of relatives and friends to whom they were given as mementos.

Mrs. Livingston was the daughter of Colonel Henry Beeckman, and her mother was either a daughter or a granddaughter of Robert Livingston, Jr., nephew of the first lord of the manor. From all lines she inherited a sound body and an active mind. Both mentally and physically she was of heroic mold. While not in any way foolhardy, it is related that she knew not fear, and she certainly was possessed of one of the most valuable gifts in the world, a keen sense of humor, which is in itself no small aid to courage. It is a tradition among all branches of the family that on the morning of this memorable flight, just as one of the first wagons was leaving the door, " Mother Margaret " burst into a hearty laugh, which broke out again at intervals all during the day — the exciting cause being the figure made by her cook, a ponderous old negro woman, perched in anxious and perilous importance on the top of a hastily packed load of provisions and kitchen utensils, and pointing her orders to her grandson, who was the acting charioteer, by wild thrusts of a long-handled toasting-fork, which by good fortune rarely hit its mark. The situation was, of course, funny enough, but most of us wait until after all danger is past before taking a proper sense of the ludicrous.

Mr. Charles H. Hunt, in his generally so accurate as well as interesting memoir of this Mrs. Livingston's youngest son,—in later years the celebrated Governor Livingston of Louisiana,— states that the destination of the party was " Salisbury, in Berkshire County, Massachusetts." Salisbury is in Connecticut, being the northwesternmost corner of that little State, where the blue Berkshire Hills smilingly refuse to acknowledge that they ever have borne allegiance to any other commonwealth.

The house in which the fugitive family was to take up its temporary abode stood very close to the boundary line of Sharon township, and was still capable of being made into a fine residence thirty-five years ago. It is melancholy to think that after remaining unoccupied for many years, being used in the meantime as a barn for hay, it has been neglected and despoiled until it is now but a dismantled ruin. As I remember it in my girlhood, the old mansion was a remarkably fine specimen of the best sort of our colonial architecture. It was built of stone and brick, of two stories and an attic above a spacious basement, a part of which probably served as a cellar, and the rest for slave quarters, as was the case in other houses of similar construction and date. At the front and rear of the second story dormer windows were set in the sides of the picturesque hipped roof. On each side of the center of a wide hall, which traversed the house from front to rear, massive chimneys ran up above the peak of the roof. The fireplaces did not open into the hall, but into the two big square rooms on the south side and the one long room on the north, which is still called the ball-room. The broad hall was beautifully wainscoted, and was adorned by a staircase which in its proportions was once a delight to the artistic eye. The ceilings of the first floor were high for that day, between ten and eleven feet, if my memory serves. All the rooms were large, finely proportioned, and admirably lighted by broad and deep windows. The ample fireplaces were surmounted by carefully finished mantelpieces of wood. I think that all the principal rooms were wainscoted, and I am sure that the window- and door-casings were of finely simple designs. The doors themselves were well paneled, thick, and strong, hung by the long-reaching hinges of wrought-iron which add so much to picturesque effect. When I saw them these had all been disfigured with paint, but my father has told me that in his youth the woodwork, of the parlor at least, was of some polished hard wood, he thought that of the cherry.

Probably not even the house she had left, though that was held to be fine in its day, was either finer or more spacious than this mansion in which Mrs.

R. R. Livingston and her family now found shelter. The house had been built by a Mr. Swift, by whom it had been sold to one of the Livingstons not very long before the opening of the war. It is not known precisely why Mr. Swift had abandoned the locality, but it is believed that he was a Royalist who had taken refuge in Boston in 1775, whence he had fled when the British abandoned that city, in company with those Tory families who sought refuge in Nova Scotia.

Just how the house came to be unoccupied at this time is not quite certain. In 1777 it belonged to Mr. Robert Livingston, the third and, save by courtesy, the last lord of the Upper Manor. He appears to have loaned the house to the Clermont party at this juncture, and at a later date he occupied it himself at intervals for short periods. Some things lead one to suppose that he and his family may have been here at the same time with the Clermont party. It is uncertain whether or not all of the last-named party stayed here through the entire winter, though some of them are known to have done so. In the following spring we find that Mrs. R. R. Livingston, with a fine confidence in the bright destinies of the struggling colonies, began to rebuild her house at Clermont. After the beginning of the summer of 1778 the house in Salisbury was occupied, more or less steadily, until after the close of the war, by the family of Robert Cambridge Livingston, the son of Robert of the Upper Manor.

I am here reminded that to readers not familiar with the subject, so many Roberts among the Livingstons may be confusing. Besides the five Robert Livingstons mentioned in this chapter, there were probably not less than a dozen more (of all ages), only to be distinguished from one another by their middle names, residences, and titles. The same was true of the Gilberts, and to nearly the same extent of the Johns and Henrys.

The life led by the refugees was both sad and joyous. On the one hand, all of them had suffered from loss and grief, and were never free from anxiety in regard to the possible fate of the dear ones in more exposed situations than their own. On the other hand, the lives of all were necessarily too laborious to leave room for idle repinings. Save for boys and old men, there were few white males left in this peaceful region. It is on record that the stated business meetings of the Congregational Society in Sharon were adjourned all through the autumn of this year, "by reason yt ye great number of men in ye service of ye Country left too few Members at home." Yet the daily needs of a large family, accustomed to every luxury of the time, were not less pressing than if there were no stress of war.

It is traditionally related of Mrs. Livingston and her daughter, Mrs. Montgomery, that they, with the aid of some of the female slaves, acted as their own coachmen and hostlers during their stay in this region, in order that their men-servants might have more time to spend in grinding meal for daily use, and in keeping the fireplaces supplied with wood. Besides this, the Clermont party joined in all the patriotic labors in which the Sharon ladies were constantly engaged. Be it remembered that stockings for the army could not be purchased in sufficient quantities, and love must be trusted to supply the want. Spinning yarn and knitting stockings, preparing bandages and scraping lint, filled every patriotic woman's every moment that could be spared from the daily cares of her family — multitudinous cares of which we now know little. Yet pleasure was mingled with them all. Our great-grandmothers were as genial and as lovable as the least burdened of their granddaughters.

Early in November, 1777, began the husking bees. A series of them was held in the biggest barn which had then been erected in Sharon or its vicinity. It belonged to Captain Simeon Smith, M.D., a physician whose military title was due to service in the campaign of 1776, on Long Island, and in the country around New York, under General Washington. This barn was taken down in my childhood, and I can just remember its wide threshing-floor, upon which horses had in the olden days been used to tread out the grain, and which was so long that five loaded hay-wagons, with horses attached, could stand in line without difficulty.

It was on this capacious threshing-floor that many of the husking frolics were held. As soon as the early November darkness had fallen, the huskers gathered from far and near. To-night it might be for Colonel Canfield's corn which had been brought here to be husked. He was with the army of Gates, and his neighbors would help both the colonel's family and their country in this humble way. Another night it might be that of some other patriot who was absent in the service of his country. It was a rule, unwritten but inflexible, that the planting and the harvests of the absent soldiers must take the precedence of those who remained at home.

Before leaving their houses all the huskers, many of whom had considerable distance to come, had partaken of as good a meal as their circumstances would permit, and all were very warmly wrapped. Good fires were kept burning in the wide fireplaces of Dr. Smith's large stone mansion, and to them the huskers often resorted, each in turn, and the work itself was warming when briskly done; but the nights were cold. The toil was made as pleasurable as possible by songs and story-telling, but the needs were too urgent to permit of loitering over it. Men and women, bond and free, boys and girls, "quality" and "commonalty," natives and refugees, all toiled together and with equal cheer and earnestness.

After the evening's task was done and all had

adjourned to the house, the different social grades sorted themselves apart and each "went to his own place." In the broad and high basement were the slave quarters, where, in front of blazing logs in wide fireplaces, they roasted potatoes in the ashes, and partook of apples, nuts, and cider, and afterward were allowed to dance until their masters summoned them to start for home. In the great kitchen, in whose fireplace an ox might have been roasted whole, another set enjoyed themselves in a similar manner; and in the generous dining-room, where a big fireplace piled high with logs of cordwood length filled the room with fragrance, warmth, and cheer, still another and probably more sumptuous repast was served.

After the supper, reels and contra-dances, where the feet beat merrily to the entrancing strains of the still traditionally remembered " Caius Tite's " fiddle, gave a sportive finish to an evening which, after all was done, had not been a long one, for all must be up and toiling again by daybreak or before. All the manor ladies and boys, as well as their servants, took a part as often as possible in these pleasurable toils. So did the city divines who shared their retreat, as well as the resident parson, though it was thought to be etiquette for them to retire to the parlors immediately after the feast, that the dance might the more speedily begin without the restraint of their presence.

CHAPTER XVII

A LITERARY CLUB IN 1779–81

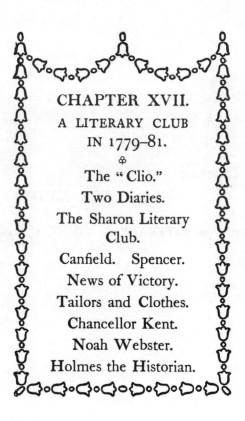

CHAPTER XVII.
A LITERARY CLUB
IN 1779–81.
♣
The "Clio."
Two Diaries.
The Sharon Literary
Club.
Canfield. Spencer.
News of Victory.
Tailors and Clothes.
Chancellor Kent.
Noah Webster.
Holmes the Historian.

WHETHER literary clubs were common things during our Revolutionary War, there are small means of knowing. The mere fact that but few traces exist does not prove that there may not have been at least one in every township, both then and for many years before, though the supposition would be against such a conclusion. So great has been the loss of old papers from fires, removals, and even wanton destruction on the part of heirs who should have known better, that the wonder is rather that we know anything of the private and social life of the colonial and Revolutionary periods than that we know so little.

In our old garret, filling a portmanteau, and perhaps left just as they were hastily stuffed into it by a young Yale College graduate in 1784, when he was quitting the college dormitory for the last time, was found a motley collection of letters, essays, translations, notes of lectures, and accounts of expenditures. Most interesting of all, for our present purpose, are two diaries and three odd copies of a manuscript publication edited by the young collegian's sister, Juliana Smith.

" The Clio, a Literary Miscellany," was legibly written in the script of different hands. The ink is still of an excellent black. The large, coarse-textured sheets of foolscap are ruled down the center of each page to form two columns, and the several sheets are tied together by cords of braided, homespun, unbleached linen thread. The three numbers are respectively dated : " December 10th, 1780," " January 30th, 1781," and " October, 1781." They contain odes, essays, proverbs, puzzles, sketches, and jokes — many of the latter being of a local coloring that has not stood the test of age. Most of the contents, particularly the sketches, would compare favorably with the larger part of the printed literary matter of the periodicals of the day. It is especially notable, considering the interest in polemics which characterized the period, that we find no reference to theological opinions.

In the same package with these manuscript magazines were several small books of a diary kept by the brother in college for the benefit of the home circle, and a larger number of little books of the same sort kept by Juliana, that her " Brother Jack " might be informed from time to time, as opportunity for transmission should serve, of the small happenings of home life. From both of these simple diaries I have gleaned many most interesting details of family and of college life, but it is principally from Juliana's lively pages that have been gathered the particulars of the literary club.

Juliana seems to have had an especially strong love both for hearing the ancestral traditions and for committing them to paper. Within the last eight or nine years my mother has told me that she had often heard her husband's grandfather — the "Brother Jack" of the diary — state that his mother and his sister Juliana were the most intellectual and the wittiest women whom he had ever known during a long life of social intercourse with the best society which our Union then afforded. They were considered especially good as narrators, and "to have coaxed either of them into telling a tale was to have provided the finest sort of an entertainment for a winter's evening." Of the correctness of this filial and fraternal judgment there is abundant evidence in the pages of both Juliana's diary and of the "Clio." The introduction, "Mamma says," is rarely prefixed to anything that is unworthy of perusal both for its own sake and for the way in which it is told, and our Juliana's signature is always to something equally good.

From the diaries we learn that the "Clio" was issued bimonthly with a praiseworthy regularity, though often the numbers could not be sent to New Haven until several had accumulated. A "post-rider" was supposed to traverse the distance between Poughkeepsie and Hartford one week, and return the next, taking in the towns of Pleasant Valley and Amenia in the State of New York, and of Sharon and Salisbury and perhaps others in Connecticut on his way; but very often, for one reason or another, he skipped a week or two, or more. The deep snows of the winters do not seem to have so frequently interfered with his progress as did the heavy freshets and fathomless mud of the springs and autumns. Probably from Hartford to New Haven the highways were kept in better order, for between these points the "Post" was much more reliable. There was also a regular post from Litchfield to New Haven, but the former place was twenty miles of bleak hill riding from Sharon. For all these reasons advantage was always taken of every private means of conveying letters. In the many thousands of letters dated prior to 1820, which I have examined, there may be found almost as many references to the unreliability of the post and the superior trustworthiness of private hands. Indeed, important letters were retained for weeks awaiting the convenience of some traveling friend "rather than to trust the Post."

Perhaps the disappearance of so many copies of the "Clio" is due to the precarious means of transportation, but, in view of the scarcity of printed periodicals, it is more likely that when the little papers were received by "brother Jack" they were passed from hand to hand until they were worn out or lost. The three surviving numbers — "One,"

"Four," and "Nineteen" — had been carefully mended to prevent them from falling to pieces.

From the "Exordium" on the first page of "No. One" it appears that "The Sharon Literary Club was founded in January, 1779, the Rev. Cotton M. Smith being Chairman and Mr. John C. Smith ["brother Jack"] being Secretary." The design of the club was "to promote a taste for the study of *Belles Lettres* and of Logick, and to gain some skill in the useful Freeman's Art of Debate." The stated meetings of the club were to be "held on every Monday evening through the Year, save from May first to October first," during which months it may be supposed that time for such pursuits could not be well spared from the pressing duties of an agriculture conducted without steam-plows, wheeled harrows, corn-planters, cultivators, mowing-machines, horse-rakes, reapers and binders, tedders and threshing-machines, to say nothing of the numberless other implements to which we are now so accustomed that we forget that Noah did not find them waiting for him when he emerged from the ark.

From the first the "Sharon Literary Club" seems to have found favor in the little township of its birth, and had continued its regular meetings from January, 1779, to May, 1780, with so much advantage that by the time for their resumption, the first Monday in the following October, it was "determined to establish The Clio so that the talents of the Club's members might be cultivated in writing as well as in speech." To its columns each club-member was "expected to make at least one contribution in every second or third number." A lawyer named Canfield (first name illegible), Mr. Ambrose Spencer, and Miss Juliana Smith were named as those "to whom all essays intended for insertion in these columns should be submitted for due consideration"; but by the time that the next surviving paper was issued, Juliana's name appears alone, although the two others continued to contribute. "Mr. Spencer," at this time a lad of about fifteen years, afterward married a daughter of Judge Canfield, and became a justice of the Supreme Court of the State of New York.

Each issue of the "Miscellany" was read aloud at the meeting of the club next after the paper's date, and as "there was much lively comment on each article," it is probable that the contents of the "Clio" formed the chief topic of the evening, after the stated reading of selected portions from certain books which the club's members were supposed to have been perusing in their own homes during the intervening days. It is interesting to know that some of these selections were translations from Cæsar's "Commentaries," made by Juliana's brother; from Plutarch's Life of Hannibal, made by the parson and the schoolmaster; and from Fénelon's "Télémaque," made by Mrs. Smith and Juliana. These translations were subject to criticism from the club's members, and on one occasion, when the learned Dr. Bellamy of Bethlehem, Connecticut, was visiting at the parsonage, there would seem to have been a good-natured but rather lively sort of a discussion between the two divines and the schoolmaster concerning the proper rendering of certain disputed passages in Plutarch. At least, Juliana reports that "they became as heated over a Greek word as if it were a forge fire."

The alternate meetings of the club were mainly debating societies, in which old and young men took part as debaters, and old and young women as listeners, while, in accordance with a resolution unanimously passed at one of the club's earliest meetings, "all of the women and such of the men as were not engaged in speaking or reading" were "expected to knit stockings or do some other work to help our brave and suffering soldiers in their desperate struggle to gain the Liberty of our Native Land." Whether shoemaking formed one of the patriotic industries pursued during these literary evenings I do not know, but presume so, for, from another source, I have found that, beginning with the winter of 1777, and onward during the war, the men of many Connecticut villages, including Sharon, "had learned to make shoes so that they might help the soldiers in the field. The State furnished the materials, and almost all the men in each township, from the Ministers down to the slaves, spent their winter evenings in making shoes for the Soldiers." It must be remembered that shoe factories were then unknown.

In spite of her silent tongue and busy fingers, at least one of the young women who were privileged to listen to the wisdom of the superior sex availed herself of her opportunities to extract abundant amusement from the readings and discussions, which she reported for the benefit of her brother and his classmates, always good-naturedly, but sometimes keenly criticizing, and in a few instances even caricaturing the speakers with an untrained but clever pencil.

It is a singular fact that neither in Juliana's diary, nor in that of her brother, nor in the surviving numbers of the "Clio," is there much mention of the war then so actively progressing. Yet Sharon was intensely patriotic, and had furnished what was, proportionately, a large contingent to the Continental forces, while the club's president had been a chaplain in the Northern army until disabled by a camp fever, and several of the most active of the club's members had been officers and privates in the patriotic armies for longer or shorter terms before 1780, and after that date still others took their places. The chief exception to this ignoring of what must have been the subject of first interest in the hearts of all is Juliana's exultation, in April, 1780, over the "sure news," which then had but just reached the little inland town,

of the victory gained the preceding September
"by Captain Paul Jones in the little Bon Homme
Richard over the big British ship Serapis. A GLO-
RIOUS VICTORY for which GOD be praised!" Perhaps the reason for the silence on the most vital
of all the topics of the time may be found in this
very thing. With the slow means of communication, suspense, long and harrowing, was inevitable. Was it not, therefore, wise to divert the
mind as much as might be while working, praying,
and hoping without cessation?

The club's meetings were "always punctually
opened at half-past seven o'clock in the evening
with a short prayer for the Divine blessing," and
they seem to have been, with equal punctuality,
closed at nine. After this refreshments were served.
If the meetings took place in almost any other
house than the parsonage, the refreshments were
followed by an hour of dancing. The sprightly
Juliana several times expresses her regret that, as
the parson's daughter, she was always obliged to
leave before the dancing began, "tho', as you
know," she once naïvely adds, "Papa does not
think dancing to be wrong in itself, but only that
it may be a cause of offending to some."

From tradition and the materials at hand we
may paint a reasonably correct picture of one of
the meetings of this long ago literary club. We
will suppose that it is held at the parsonage. Here
three rooms are opened to the company — the

parson's study, the family living-room, and the kitchen. In all three great blazing logs of wood are sending their cheerful heat and light principally up the broad-throated chimneys. The night is very cold, but the guests do not feel its chill too acutely, for the air of the rooms is so fresh that the blood is well oxygenated. The curtains, too, are closely drawn, and they are not flimsy things, but thick and heavy, made to keep the wind out, and they are drawn over doors as well as windows. Such curtains are usually made of a mixture of linen and wool, homespun, home-dyed, and home-woven, and were sometimes lined and quilted. In the wealthiest families curtains of flowered chintz were often hung on the roomward side of the heavier curtains, and sometimes, but probably very seldom, they were all displaced by imported satin-damask or damask-moreen, lined with wadded and quilted silk.

Even at this late period there would not be enough chairs to seat all the guests, for these, in Juliana's reports to her brother, are often said to number more than one hundred; so the forms were brought from the schoolhouse, and were sometimes supplemented by long planks laid from one stool or block of wood to another.

As both the study and the living-room communicated with the kitchen, which extended along the house at the rear of both of them, and a speaker or reader standing midway of the kitchen could easily be heard in both of the other rooms, it is probable that here would be the chosen position.

There would be some finely dressed persons present, for at this time there were gentlemen and ladies of fortune and position in this retired spot, safe from war's alarms, and they would be attired as became their station; but the most would be arrayed in clothes of home manufacture, from pocket-handkerchief to shoe-tie. Tailors were so few that well-fitting coats and breeches must have been rare. One unfortunate college student from this neighborhood had placed the cloth for a suit of clothes with the local tailor in the spring, and by the time that potentate had seen fit to finish them, the garments had been so far outgrown that they had to be passed over to a younger brother; and the same thing was repeated twice, so that the poor student must have been agonizing in out-grown or out-worn clothes for the greater part of his college course. For this state of things there was no help. The tailor, having no competitor within thirty miles in any direction, was monarch of his customers. Storm and threaten they never so sternly, they were obliged to wait his pleasure, for they could get no better served even by journeying long distances. The trade of the tailor, however profitable, was despised in the colonies, and few would engage in it. Consequently, during the years preceding the war, the larger part of the wearing apparel of even wealthy men was either imported from England, as made to order from more or less accurate measurements, or was of household manufacture. The same was true of much of the dress of the women; but in their case it would not so greatly matter, as the materials were so much more pliable, and the custom of wearing an abundance of lace trimmings on the gowns of the young, and of covering the neck and shoulders of the elderly with crossed kerchiefs or small shawls, concealed a multitude of defects. During the war such imported clothes as existed must have been decidedly old in style, but that would have been too universal to have been noticeable.

Gaiety there must have been in plenty. There could have been little dullness where such mirthful spirits as Juliana, her sister Elizabeth, and their mother were the leaders, and this they plainly were, notwithstanding that they " maintained a seemly silence while the slower half of creation was laying down the law."

Both from the pages of the "Clio" itself and from those of Juliana's diary, which, with comparatively few breaks, was continued all through her " brother Jack's " four years in Yale, there is abundant evidence that the literary instinct in that quiet village, then so very remote from all the centers of activity, was by no means confined to the family in the parsonage, though its manifestations were led from there.

The club's meetings were held in various houses, from the stately " Montgomery House " on the hill dividing Salisbury from Sharon, which was occupied by one or another of the numerous branches of the Livingston families during nearly the entire war, to the brick cottage occupied by the families of Robert G. Livingston and the lately deceased Philip Livingston, which was on one side of the parsonage, and to the broadly spreading house of Judge Canfield on its other side.   In all, seventeen dwellings are mentioned as having at one time or another been meeting-places for the club.   Several of these still exist, but only three of them are now occupied by the heirs of the then owners.   These three are the " Gay House," more than a mile above the village, the " King House," at the head of the beautiful village street, and the " Smith House," in whose garret are the papers from which we quote.   All are in good preservation and are fine specimens of colonial architecture.

Juliana evidently possessed a good degree of literary and editorial instinct.   From the lips of her two grandmothers and from her mother — herself too busy to spend much time in writing — the young lady obtained many narratives of early days in the colonies.   To several of these she incidentally refers, and some of them she wrote at considerable length in her diary for Jack's benefit. From these narratives she sometimes made such extracts as she deemed suitable for the " Clio," though not as often as she (and we) would have liked, because, as she writes to Jack : "Judge Canfield seems to think that such things foster pride and vanity, albeit, *Nota Bene*, I think I do observe now and then a morsel of those sinful emotions in himself. Dost remember him, dear Jack ? "

From her brother and his classmates Juliana was indefatigable in begging contributions, whether in prose or in verse, declaring that she "cared less for moral reflections than for new thoughts," and that "most of all" she desired "news and narratives of things that one has not already heard or read a thousand times. Of course," she adds, " Odes and Sonnets would be very fine IF they were *poetical*, but, Oh, my dear Jack, I fear me there is very little promise that any of your Friends will prove to be Shakespeares or Miltons."

It must be confessed that the most of the surviving contributions of the young collegians are decidedly sophmoric in tone, and we cannot blame the editress, who does not hesitate to inform Jack, by way of consolation after some sharp criticisms, that she "hopes, nay, believes, that he will be wiser by-and-bye"; and, after reading a certain halting "Ode" by A. H., we are ready to confirm the editorial opinion that " your chum " (Abiel Holmes, afterward author of the laborious " Annals of American History," but better known as the father of Oliver Wendell Holmes) " is no doubt, as you say, a Man of Parts, but the Pegasus he rides is a sorry steed that has lost his wings and is badly shod." Of James Kent, afterward the justly celebrated Chancellor Kent of the State of New York, she says: "Mr. Kent does well, always well. He has thoughts and does not hide them under a rubbish heap of words as H—s and S. B. do. . . . I wish that your friend Daggett" (David Daggett, afterward United States senator from Connecticut for several terms, and a judge of high standing) "would be so obliging as to be a more frequent contributor; he writes wittily and without affectation."

One contribution in a surviving number of the "Clio" is signed "Noah Webster." The future lexicographer was then teaching a district school in Sharon, and "boarding round," receiving the extravagant salary of three dollars a month. This I find from the private account-book of the acting town clerk, through whom the stipend was paid. The somewhat hackneyed moral lesson which Mr. Webster wished to convey was cast in the dream form which seems to have appealed so strongly to the fancy of the age, and is a stilted, disjointed sort of thing; yet it hardly deserved the little fling of the young editress — herself, it will be remembered, only nineteen:

"Mr. Webster has not the excuse of youth, (I think he must be fully twenty two or three), but his essays — don't be angry, Jack,— are as young

as yours or brother Tommy's, while his reflections
are as prosy as those of our horse, your namesake,
would be if they were written out. Perhaps more
so, for I truly believe, judging from the way *Jack
Horse* looks round at me sometimes, when I am on
his back, that his thoughts of the human race and
their conduct towards his own, might be well
worth reading. At least they would be all *his own*,
and that is more than can be said of N. W.'s. . . .
In conversation he is even duller than in writing,
if that be possible, but he is a painstaking man
and a hard student. Papa says he will make his
mark; but then, you know that our dear Papa is
always inclined to think the best of every one's
abilities, *except* his own and MINE, of which last, I
grieve to say, his opinion seems to be sadly low.
Perhaps that is because every one says I am so
like him; you know he is ever repeating that self-
praise is no credit! I wish *you* were at home, dear
Jack, so that I might get a word of flattery now
and then. I would pay you back in your own
coin! "

A club-member whose contributions pleased the
critical Juliana much better than those of the
future lexicographer was a Mr. Beecher, who was
in some way related to the subsequently celebrated
Rev. Lyman Beecher. He was perhaps a brother
of the latter's father. None of his papers appear
in the still-existing numbers of the " Clio," and

perhaps he did not write many, but he was always
an active member of the club. "Mr. Beecher is,"
says Juliana, "the life of our Debates. Every
thing he utters is to the point, forcible, pungent,
and often so witty that we are in convulsions of
laughter. Papa says he is one who would become
great, an he had the opportunity. As it is, though
he is not great, he well fills his lot in life and is
somewhat of a power in our little community."
In another place she writes: "Mr. Beecher was
on what I conceive to be the wrong side of the
question last night, but I must concede that his
remarks were full of force, fire and persuasion.
What a pity that he could not receive the advantages which are now being, as it seems to me,
wasted on P. L. Jr! I believe that Mr. B. would
make a preacher of extraordinary eloquence."

On at least one occasion there was present a
young surgeon of the Continental troops, probably
home on leave of absence. Dr. Wheeler, afterward of Redhook on the Hudson, may have been
drawn to Sharon by the charms of Elizabeth,
Juliana's sister, whom he subsequently married,
but where they first met does not appear. In 1782
we find in Juliana's diary the first mention of one
who not long after became the controlling influence
in her life. "This evening," she says, "our debates were enlivened by the presence of a young
gentleman who came in with Judge Canfield and
his daughters. He is very handsome in person and

courtly in manners. His remarks were received with much favor, even the *carping* P. L. being heard to say that Mr. Radcliff's speech 'was not intolerable.' I fear me he would not have conceded as much to one of ourselves. Mr. L. never has any faith in home born prophets."

After this, Mr. Radcliff's name is mentioned a good many times, but — or at least so it seems in the light of future events — with an ever-increasing reticence. Whatever may have been the occasion which first drew the young gentleman to Sharon, there is no doubt that the reason for subsequent visits was to be found in the attractions of the handsome and quick-witted Juliana. Until after the peace the time was not propitious for members of the legal profession, and the betrothed couple had to spend two and perhaps more years of happy, hopeful waiting. Almost immediately after the peace young Mr. and Mrs. Jacob Radcliff began to live in Albany, New York, where in time he became one of the judges of the Supreme Court of Judicature. At a later period they removed to New York city, of which Mr. Radcliff was mayor for three terms between 1810 and 1818.

Apparently from about 1790 the Radcliffs had a summer home on the banks of the Hudson. "Chestnut Hill" was not far from Poughkeepsie. At this home Mr. and Mrs. Radcliff entertained largely and handsomely, and the name of the hostess is often mentioned in domestic chronicles of that date as that of one of the most charming members of the notedly charming society which gathered along the banks of what used then to be so affectionately termed " the River." The " literary evenings at the Radcliffs of Chestnut Hill " are mentioned in published and in unpublished letters written by Chancellor Kent, Edward Livingston, Chancellor Livingston, and Mrs. Janet Montgomery, as stated and delightful gatherings where youth and age, fashion and wit, met for pleasure and improvement. It is not too much to assume that the idea for these gatherings was taken from the literary club which had been so great a social and mental resource to the members of an inland country parson's parish at an earlier date.

Tradition tells us that after the marriage of the young editress the " Clio " ceased to appear, but that the club continued in active operation for twenty or more years later. I have found no record of this, but in a few instances certain allusions in private correspondence countenance tradition.

It has several times been affirmed that the first purely literary club in the United States was the one which was started by Mrs. Lydia H. Sigourney in Hartford, Connecticut, in the early years of the present century. Our records prove that the one in Sharon was very much earlier, and it is probable that others had preceded it; but until some other claimant shall arise we may continue to give to the beautiful little village of Sharon, Connecticut, the honor of being the mother of literary clubs in the United States.

CHAPTER XVIII

NEW ENGLAND'S FESTIVE DAY

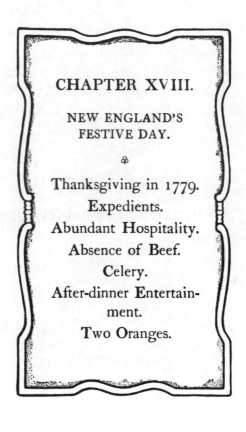

CHAPTER XVIII.

NEW ENGLAND'S
FESTIVE DAY.

♣

Thanksgiving in 1779.
Expedients.
Abundant Hospitality.
Absence of Beef.
Celery.
After-dinner Entertain-
ment.
Two Oranges.

THE following account of a Thanksgiving dinner in 1779 is given in a letter of Juliana Smith's, copied by her into her diary — a praiseworthy practice not uncommon when letters were written with care and might easily be lost in transmission. This letter was addressed to its writer's "Dear Cousin Betsey." Who the latter may have been I do not know, but presume that she was a daughter of the Rev C. M. Smith's elder brother Dan.

After the usual number of apologies for delay in writing, Juliana proceeds:

"When Thanksgiving Day was approaching our dear Grandmother Smith [*née* Jerusha Mather, great-granddaughter of the Rev. Richard Mather of Dorchester, Massachusetts], who is sometimes a little desponding of Spirit as you well know, did her best to persuade us that it would be better to make it a Day of Fasting & Prayer in view of the *Wickedness of our Friends & the Vileness of our Enemies*, I am sure you can hear Grandmother say that and see her shake her cap border. But indeed there was some occasion for her remarks, for our resistance to an *unjust Authority* has cost our beautiful Coast Towns very dear the last year & all of us have had much to suffer. But my dear Father brought her to a more proper frame of Mind, so that by the time the Day came she was ready to enjoy it almost as well as Grandmother Worthington did, & she, you will remember, always sees the bright side. In the mean while we had all of us been working hard to get all things in readiness to do honour to the Day.

" This year it was Uncle Simeon's turn to have the dinner at his house, but of course we all helped them as they help us when it is our turn, & there is always enough for us all to do. All the baking of pies & cakes was done at our house & we had the big oven heated & filled twice each day for three days before it was all done. & *everything was* GOOD, though we did have to do without some things that ought to be used. Neither Love nor (paper) Money could buy Raisins, but our good red cherries dried without the pits, did almost as well & happily Uncle Simeon still had some spices in store. The tables were set in the Dining Hall and even that big room had no space to spare when we were all seated. The Servants had enough ado to get around the Tables & serve us all without over-setting things. There were our two Grandmothers side by side. They are always handsome old Ladies, but now, many thought, they were handsomer than ever, & happy they were to look around upon so many of their descendants. Uncle & Aunt Simeon presided at one Table, & Father & Mother at the other. Besides us five boys & girls there were two of the Gales & three Elmers, besides James Browne & Ephraim Cowles. [Five of the last-named seven were orphans taught and in all ways provided for by Parson & Mrs. Smith.] We had them at our table because they could be best *supervised* there. Most of the students had gone to their own homes for the week, but Mr. Skiff & Mr. —— [name illegible] were too far away from their homes. They sat at Uncle Simeon's table & so did Uncle Paul & his family, five of them in all, & Cousins Phin & Poll [probably Phineas and Apollos Smith, sons of Dan]. Then there were six of the Livingston family next door. They had never seen a Thanksgiving Dinner before, having been used to keep Christmas Day instead, as is the wont in New York Province. Then there were four Old Ladies who have no longer Homes or Children of their own & so came to us. They were invited by my Mother, but Uncle and Aunt Simeon wished it so.

" Of course we could have no Roast Beef. None of us have tasted Beef this three years back as it all must go to the Army, & too little they get, poor fellows. But, Nayquittymaw's Hunters were able to get us a fine red Deer, so that we had a good haunch of Venisson on each Table. These were balanced by huge Chines of Roast Pork at the other ends of the Tables. Then there was on one a big Roast Turkey & on the other a Goose, & two big Pigeon Pasties. Then there was an abundance of good Vegetables of all the old Sorts & one which I do not believe you have yet seen. Uncle Simeon had imported the Seede from England just before the War began & only this Year was there enough for Table use. It is called Sellery & you eat it without cooking. It is very good served with meats. Next year Uncle Simeon says he will be able to raise enough to give us all some. It has to be taken up, roots & all & buried in earth in the cellar through the winter & only pulling up some when you want it to use.

"Our Mince Pies were good although we had to use dried Cherries as I told you, & the meat was shoulder of Venisson, instead of Beef. The Pumpkin Pies, Apple Tarts & big Indian Puddings lacked for nothing save *Appetite* by the time we had got round to them.

"Of course we had no Wine. Uncle Simeon has still a cask or two, but it must all be saved for the sick, & indeed, for those who are well, good Cider is a sufficient Substitute. There was no Plumb Pudding, but a boiled Suet Pudding, stirred thick with dried Plumbs & Cherries, was called by the old Name & answered the purpose.

All the other spice had been used in the Mince
Pies, so for this Pudding we used a jar of West
India preserved Ginger which chanced to be left
of the last shipment which Uncle Simeon had from
there, we chopped the Ginger small and stirred it
through with the Plumbs & Cherries. It was
extraordinary good. The Day was bitter cold &
when we got home from Meeting, which Father
did not keep over long by reason of the cold, we
were glad eno' of the fire in Uncle's Dining Hall,
but by the time the dinner was one half over
those of us who were on the fire side of one Table
was forced to get up & carry our plates with us
around to the far side of the other Table, while those
who had sat there were as glad to bring their plates
around to the fire side to get warm. All but the
Old Ladies who had a screen put behind their
chairs."

Here it may be allowed to break in upon Juliana's narrative to explain that the hall in which
this dinner was laid, now long used as a kitchen,
is a room about thirty feet long from north to
south and twenty-two feet wide. A glazed door
and a window open upon piazzas from each
end. On the western side a broadly hospitable
door opens into the staircase hall of the main
building, while in the dining-room itself another
flight of stairs ascended from the same side to the
wing's chambers. On the eastern side is the im-

mense chimney, where once yawned a fireplace that " would comfortably hold a full sled load of eight foot logs." With such a fire it is no wonder that the guests seated near it were glad to exchange places with the others, who — probably half freezing — were on the other side of the room. When I was about seven or eight years old. the heavy ceiling beams, darkened with age and smoke, were hidden away from view by a plaster ceiling. I pleaded in vain for the " pretty brown beams " to be left in sight, but my grandmother was inflexible, and no doubt, in the interest of comfort for her servants, she was quite right to close the drafty fireplace and lower the lofty ceiling. Nevertheless it was a pity, and I have never ceased to regret it.

"Uncle Simeon," proceeds Juliana, "was in his best mood, and you know how good that is! He kept both Tables in a roar of laughter with his droll stories of the days when he was studying medicine in Edinborough, & afterwards he & Father & Uncle Paul joined in singing Hymns & Ballads. You know how fine their voices go together. Then we all sang a Hymn & afterwards my dear Father led us in prayer, remembering all Absent Friends before the Throne of Grace, & much I wished that my dear Betsey was here as one of us, as she has been of yore.

"We did not rise from the Table until it was quite dark, & then when the dishes had been cleared away we all got round the fire as close as we could, & cracked nuts, & sang songs & told stories. At least some told & others listened. *You know nobody* can exceed the two Grandmothers at telling tales of all the things they have seen themselves, & repeating those of the early years in New England, & even some in the Old England, which they had heard in their youth from their Elders. My Father says it is a goodly custom to hand down all worthy deeds & traditions from Father to Son, as the Israelites were commanded to do about the Passover & as the Indians here have always done, because the Word that is spoken is remembered longer than the one that is written. . . . Brother Jack, who did not reach here until late on Wednesday though he had left College very early on Monday Morning & rode with all due diligence considering the snow, brought an orange to each of the Grand-Mothers, but, Alas! they were frozen in his saddle bags. We soaked the frost out in cold water, but I guess they was n't as good as they should have been."

CHAPTER XIX

A SNOW-SHOE JOURNEY

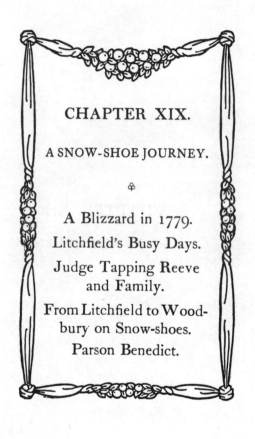

CHAPTER XIX.

A SNOW-SHOE JOURNEY.

ॐ

A Blizzard in 1779.
Litchfield's Busy Days.

Judge Tapping Reeve
and Family.

From Litchfield to Wood-
bury on Snow-shoes.
Parson Benedict.

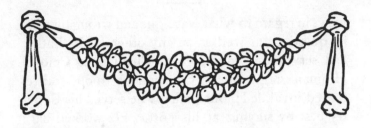

"ROTHER JACK " has left among his papers a relation, written in 1844, for the benefit of his grandchildren, in which he refers to the same Thanksgiving day of which Juliana wrote, but dwells more particularly upon the return journey to New Haven, on which his father accompanied him. He writes:

" After the day of praise and feasting came two days of visiting pleasantly among our neighbors, all of whom made themselves very agreeable to me as one who had come from a far country. On Sunday there were two services, which, I suppose would now be called very long, though my Father would never allow himself to preach as long sermons as were then customary, unless carried away by his feelings, which sometimes happened when the news from the posts of danger was recent and exciting. There was no hesitation about preaching political sermons in those days. Ministers would have deemed themselves to have entirely failed of their duty, had they not expressed their views in regard to what was right and wrong on public questions as well as on any other. My Father had served one campaign as Chaplain to Colonel Hinman's regiment of Connecticut troops and returned invalided; but perhaps he served his Country best by staying at his post. He worked hard both in his own harvest fields and in those of his parishoners to raise grain for the armies; he cared for the families of those who were at the front, and he helped to keep the fires of patriotism glowing by his exhortations from the pulpit.

" Although early in the season the sleighing had already been good for a fortnight, and the snow was again falling when we set out very early on Monday morning, my Father and I, in our big box sleigh, well wrapped in robes of long wooled sheep-skins, and drawn by two old farm horses, not the best because the best had gone to the army. Fine as the sleighing was in the immediate neighborhood of Sharon, we found the roads badly drifted long before we reached what is now Ellsworth. At that point, only about five miles from home, we had to leave our sleigh in the care of one of my Father's parishoners, while we pursued our journey on horseback. In those days no one travelled in any sort of a vehicle without taking along saddles for use in emergency. It was dark before we reached Litchfield and the snow-laden wind was piercingly cold.

" Judge Tapping Reeve, though much younger

than my Father, was one of the latter's choice
friends, and it was at his home that by previous
arrangement we were to pass the night. Judge
Reeve was both a good and a great man as well as
one of the most eloquent speakers who ever
adorned the Bar of his own or any other State.
Five years later than this I was one of the earliest
students in his law-school, started in 1784, and
since become so famous. From it have been
graduated upwards of one hundred lawyers, among
them being some of our most distinguished
statesmen.

" It was on this delightful evening, when we
were all sitting round the roaring fire in the broad
fire-place of Mrs. Reeve's pleasant sitting room,
and while we were listening to the elevating conversation between Judge Reeve and my Father,
that I made up my mind that the Law should be
my profession. Before this time I had hesitated,
but now I felt sure that an honest man could do
as much good in this profession as in any other.
My Father and the Judge fully coincided in senti-
ment, especially in wishing to supercede by a better that portion of the old English Common Law
which takes away all property rights from married
women. Both of them had shown their faith by
their works. Both my Mother and Mrs. Reeve
had inherited small fortunes and had been allowed
by their husbands to retain the control of their own
property ; a thing almost unheard of at that time in

cases where no ante-nuptial settlements had been made. The views of both men as I heard them stated at this time were afterwards clearly set forth by Judge Reeve in his celebrated pamphlet on 'The Domestic Relations.' This was the first voice ever publicly raised in our country, and perhaps in any other, in behalf of the property rights of married women, and attracted much attention both favourable and unfavourable. Judge Reeve stood almost alone on this point among the lawyers of his day; but in his school he made many disciples.

"Mrs. Reeve also took a part in this discussion and fully vindicated her right to do so by the intellectual ability she manifested as might be expected from a person of her lineage. Judge Reeve was always noted as a model husband and it was no wonder with such a wife as his. Mrs. Reeve was sister to Colonel Aaron Burr, and possessed all the latter's great intellectual powers and wonderful personal attractions without one of his faults. She was nearly always in delicate health which forced her to lead a very secluded life, but she had every qualification to have placed her among those women who have been most noted for goodness, grace, beauty and wit.

"I seem to myself to see her now as she appeared that night. She was still but a young matron and in the full flush of a beauty that was less of feature than of expression. I thought then and I think now, that Mrs. Reeve was one of those women to whom it is an honour to any man to bow in deference. She had inherited the faculty of close logic which distinguished her Grandfather, the great Dr. Jonathan Edwards, and the persuasive grace of her Father, the Rev. Dr. Burr, of Princeton. She was small and slight, with a dazzling complexion, clear cut features and deep gray eyes that under any intellectual excitement became brilliant. Her smile was irresistible. At least it so seemed to me on that first interview when I was but fourteen years of age. Afterwards, during the years that I studied in Judge Reeve's office and had my home in his household, the impression became fixed, and I believe it was the same with every succeeding student who had the privilege of being admitted into that family circle.

" During the night the storm increased in violence and in the morning it was impossible to see many feet from the door on account of the whirling masses of a snow so hard, dry and powdery that it cut into the face like fine iron filings. To proceed on our journey was clearly impossible. Neither man nor beast could long have endured the intense cold and the friction of the icy snow, even if it had been possible for any one to keep the direction in the blinding storm. In traversing the short distance from the house to the barn to attend to the wants of our animals, over a path hardly more than twenty yards long and partly sheltered by the wood-shed, we were almost blinded and bewildered.

"All that day and far into the night of Tuesday we piled logs upon the kitchen fire, for in that room alone was it possible to maintain a comfortable degree of warmth. Fortunately there was space enough for us all to sit without disturbing the labours of the servants in preparing our meals. As no one could be allowed to remain idle in such times of pressing need, my Father and I helped to mould bullets for the soldiers' muskets, while gentle Mrs. Reeve sat busily knitting on yarn stockings for their feet. The wind blew so fiercely down through all the other chimneys in the house that it was impossible to light the fires in them. It is under such circumstances that characters are displayed without disguise, and Judge and Mrs. Reeve then seemed, what I afterwards proved them to be, genial, courteous and kind: making light of every difficulty, and by their hearty warmth of welcome and their sparkling wit making that day and evening among the happiest recollections of a lifetime which has held as many joys and as few sorrows as may fall to the lot of mortals.

"On Wednesday the sun rose bright and clear over a dazzling desert of snow. The lower windows of most of the houses were hidden beneath great piles of drift. In some cases even the second story windows were hidden, or only visible through openings in the drift like the hooded bastions of some icy fort. Looking from the garret windows of Judge Reeve's house as far as the eye could reach we could see no trace of road or path. Fences and shrubs were obliterated. Trees, some looking like mountains of snow and some like naked and broken skeletons, arose here and there. And in the village only rising wreaths of smoke told that life existed in the half buried houses. The Meeting House spire was on one side decked by the icy snow with fantastic semblances of marble statuary over which the new long, black lightning rod (the first one I had ever seen) had been twisted by the wind until it looked like a Chinese character. The Meeting House, where on Sunday the Rev. Judah Champion thundered his rousing appeals to the patriotism of his congregation; the great house for the reception of military stores on North Street, and the Army Work-Shop, where blacksmiths, gunsmiths and the makers of saddles and harness were constantly working for the troops, were the only buildings which were large enough to serve as land-marks to any but the natives of the place under this bewildering confusion of snow. The military guard which was always stationed to protect these valuable buildings, on this day omitted their customary drills to take their places in the 'Shovel Brigade' which was organized to dig out the beleagured inhabitants. One might suppose that we were in Lapland or Iceland, so strange and frozen did everything look; so vast seemed the desert of snow which even on a level was found to be several feet in depth and was everywhere covered with a frozen crust.

"'Now we shall have the pleasure of keeping you for a week at least,' said Judge Reeve, heartily clasping my Father's hand.

"'Yes,' said dear Mrs. Reeve, giving me a kindly look, 'yes, my dear boy, you will not get back to your classes this week.'

"I was both enchanted and miserable. To stay in this beautiful home would be most delightful. To lose the time from my classes would be almost unendurable. My Father settled the matter by asking quietly if our host could not get us each a pair of snow shoes.

"At first our hosts treated this request as a pleasantry, but when they perceived that my Father was quite in earnest their dismay was amusing. The general habit of using snow shoes, which at a very early period had been adopted from the Indians, had already nearly disappeared, but down to a comparatively recent period there had been a few persons who continued to use them in places where there were no interruptions from fences. My Father, a slight but sinewy and most athletic man, had spent two or three years of his early life as teacher in a school which had been recently established for the instruction of Indians in Stockbridge, Massachusetts, and there he had joined in all the athletic sports of the natives, gaining a great influence among them by his prowess in running, leaping and wrestling. (It has nothing to do with our present purpose, but my descendants may like to know that the marks reached by my Father, when a student at Yale, for running and standing leaps, were kept as the highest attained by any student on the college Campus. No one else had been able to reach the same until I did so in my Senior year.)

"It was among the Indians that my Father had learned to use the snow shoes with great skill and as much grace as the unwieldy things would permit, but I could never see him or any one else on them without an inclination to laugh which was sometimes stronger than my filial reverence. But, as my Father had a strong vein of humour, he always rather joined in my mirth than rebuked me for it. Fore-seeing that there might be some occasion on which this somewhat unusual accomplishment might prove of service, my Father had taught me also to become moderately expert in the use of snow shoes.

"Fortunately Judge Reeve had stored away in his garret, more as a curiosity than for any use that he expected to be made of them, two pairs of snow shoes of the finest Indian manufacture, so that we had not to spend any time in searching for them, and by nine o'clock on Wednesday morn-

ing we climbed out of an upper story window upon
the hard crust of frozen snow and started off with
no other burden than the light, but cumbersome
snow shoes attached to our feet, and a small roll
like a knapsack, fastened to each of our backs.

" I was a boy of unusual strength for my years,
and my Father, although a Parson, was remarkable
for his vigor, but I can assure you that we were
both of us thankful when at nightfall we reached
the little town of Bethlehem and the hospitable
abode of my Father's very dear friend, the Rev.
Dr. Joseph Bellamy. Although the distance is a
little more than ten miles as the crow flies, it had
seemed a long journey and I had never been so
tired before.

" On Thursday the roads continuing impassable
we could not abandon our snow shoes, though they
made our ankles ache so that we could hardly
stand upon them. The air was of a clear, still
cold that would have been severe if we had not
been exercising ourselves so greatly. Even as it
was our dread-naughts [these were caped coats of
exceedingly thick homespun cloth, belted around
the waist and descending well below the knees]
were none too warm.

" Our second day's journey on the snow shoes
was much like the first, and of about the same
length, bringing us to Woodbury and the house
of the Rev. Noah Benedict where we were entertained with warm hospitality. Mr. Benedict was

a peace making man in his congregation, and his gentle spirit long influenced the manners and the actions of the people of his flock. But in public matters he was as war-like as any of us. Woodbury, like Litchfield, was a place for the collection and storage of the supplies for the patriot armies. Here we found the streets, running each way from the Meeting House, piled high on either side for a hundred yards or more with barrels and hogsheads of pork, beef, lard and flour, besides great quantities of bales of blankets, tents and clothing for the troops. All these now made miniature mountains under the snow. Almost all the able bodied male inhabitants more than seventeen years of age were enrolled in the armies, and the work pertaining to the stores was carried on by the women and children under the direction of a few old men. Many shoes were made in this place for the troops. Parson Benedict had himself been taught to make them that he might assist in the work. On this evening the women of the family were paring apples to dry for the army use and as my Father and I could not assist Mr. Benedict and the men servants in shoemaking we took our part in the apple paring. And a very merry and delightful evening we all had together, for to work with a good will is a sure road to happiness, let our circumstances be as untoward as they may.

"Friday morning found the temperature greatly modified, and, by the time we had accomplished the first five or six miles of our journey toward New Haven we found ourselves in an evil case, for the snow was beginning to get wet and soft and held down the four foot length of snow shoe so that at every step it became harder to lift our feet. Glad enough were we when at last we reached an inn where the accommodations were poor enough, but where we could at least get a little refreshment for ourselves and were able to leave the snow shoes to await some later opportunity to be returned to Judge Reeve, and to hire horses to ride upon to New Haven. From this point the snow was not nearly so deep and we had but little trouble in making, by eight in the evening, the eighteen miles to the house of the Rev. Dr. Daggett, the venerable ex-President of Yale College ; which house was almost a second home to us.

" Tired as I had been the day before, I found myself still more so to-night; but my Father would not allow me to complain, saying that I should never make a soldier who could serve his country, as our soldiers were now doing, if I gave out so easily. Never-the-less, I observed that my Father was himself very lame for the next few days and by no means in haste to depart for home again as he would otherwise have been. I have never regretted the experience,— since no harm save a few days of stiff joints and sore bones came of it,— but I think that my Mother's remark when she heard of it showed much common sense:—

" 'A week or two more or less would not have spoiled our Johnny's prospects, and lung fevers might have destroyed both your lives. *I say, leave Indian ways to Indian folk.*'

" 'Never-the-less,' answered my Father, with a merry twinkle in the eye, 'never-the-less, my dear, I observe that when you have anything to do you brook no delays and you shirk no labour. Your wisdom seems rather to be for others than for yourself.'

"My Mother shook her head slightly and walked away, turning to say over her shoulder,— 'And would you have the Great-granddaughter of Captain John Gallup any more timorsome than her husband?'"

CHAPTER XX

A NEW YORK EVENING FROLIC

CHAPTER XX.

A NEW YORK EVENING FROLIC.

✠

Mr. David Codwise Tells
of an Evening at the
Rhinelander Homestead.
Candles and Candle-
dipping.
The Supper.
The " Fire Dance."
The Parting Cup.

IN 1796 Mr. David Codwise, my great-uncle by his marriage with my paternal grandmother's sister, Martha Livingston, was a boy of sixteen and a student in Columbia College. When he gave me the following story of an evening's frolic he was about eighty-two, in an "anecdotage" which rendered him very interesting to at least one of his frequent listeners. He was a lifelong resident of his native city, and knew the history of every important building and person in it, but among all his narratives few interested me more than that of the "candle-dip frolic."

Among the masses of old papers in my possession I find no trace of the use of lamps for burning any sort of oil previous to 1760. This, of course, does not prove that they did not exist, but only that probably candles were the chief illuminating power. In bills of household supplies I find always a certain quantity of wax candles, but the imported article at four English shillings the pound (in 1762) must obviously have been kept for festive occasions only. It is probable that the wax from the combs of both the wild and the domestic bees was used for home-made mold candles, as in New England was also the wax from the green and fragrant bayberries; but the main dependence must have been the tallow dips, and even these could not have been very freely used by any but the well-to-do. Tallow candles were not superseded by wax even in the Grand Opera House of Paris until during the Regency, 1715–23.

Candle-dipping was one of the employments of every winter, and sometimes became an enjoyment also. The special candle-dipping of which my uncle told was at the home of a certain Miss Rhinelander, for whom he ever retained a tender memory.

The scene was an immense kitchen. Between the heavy ceiling beams, darkened and polished by the years of kindly smoke, hung bunches of dried herbs and of ears of corn for popping. A large portion of one side of the room was taken up by a fireplace so big that there was space for a seat at each end after piles of logs four or five feet in length had begun to send their blaze up the wide chimney throat. These seats were stone slabs set in the side walls of the fireplace, and — as seats — were only used by persons who came in literally dripping with rain or melting snow. Usually the slabs were employed as resting-places for things to be kept hot without burning. Adjoining the fireplace was the great brick oven. Over the blaze swung long-armed cranes supporting immense brass kettles, their outsides already blackening with smoke, although only a few hours earlier they had been scoured to a dazzling brightness. The floor, "as white as a wooden trencher," was sprinkled with shining sand. Mr. Codwise did not remember that there was any light beyond that supplied by the blazing logs. The whitewashed walls were decorated with evergreen boughs.

Down the center, the longest way of the room, were two long ladders lying side by side, supported at either end upon blocks of wood about "chair-seat high." Under each ladder, at intervals of a foot or so apart, stood a row of big three-footed iron pots and of footless brass kettles like those over the fire. On the floor, between the pots and the kettles, were placed dripping-pans and other vessels, both to protect the floor from grease and to prevent waste of tallow. On either side of each recumbent ladder was a row of chairs, placed as closely together as possible. Before the merrymakers were seated — John by Molly and Peter by Sally — big and jolly black Castor and Pollux had lifted from the fire the brass kettles full of melted tallow, and deftly poured their contents to the depth of two or three inches more than a long candle's length upon the water with which the similar vessels on the floor were already half filled.

As soon as the young folks were seated, black Phyllis and Chloe, dressed in butternut homespun with white kerchiefs over the shoulders, and wearing red-and-yellow plaided turbans, deftly handed the candle rods, four or five to each person. From each rod were suspended the wicks of twisted cotton yarn which it had been the task of the young lady hostess and her friends to prepare during the previous afternoon.

The first dippings were rather solemn affairs. Much depended upon starting right. The least crook in the wick, if not straightened, insured a crooked candle; and crooked candles were drippy things, burning unevenly, and guttering in a way most vexatious to the good housewife. About six wicks were upon each rod. They must not hang too closely together, or, like too thickly planted trees, they would interfere with each other as they grew. They must not be too far apart, or there would not be room enough for all to be plunged evenly in the kettles. The wicks on each rod were dipped carefully their entire length in the kettle nearest to the right hand of the person dipping, the wicks necessarily passing through the melted tallow resting on top of the water, and acquiring with each dip a thin layer of the tallow. The tallow in the kettles was frequently replenished, that the wicks might never be allowed to touch the water, lest a spluttering candle should result. Candle-dipping must not be retarded, and it could not be hurried. Slowly the wicks were immersed in the tallow, and then the loaded rods were hung in the spaces between the kettles and over the empty pans to allow the growing candles to harden before being dipped again and again until the proper circumference had been attained.

Probably two pairs of industrious hands, having six kettles between them, could easily have completed as many candles in three hours as six pairs could have done under the merrymaking conditions; but then, where would have been the fun of the thing? There is an old Dutch proverb to the effect that "life's employments are life's enjoyments," and there is abundant proof that our happily constituted Dutch ancestors made enjoyments of the most prosaic employments. Certainly there was pleasure enough at this candle-dipping frolic, in the house of a wealthy citizen, and attended by the youthful élite of the little city only one century ago. Their present-day successors can get no more at no matter what may be the chosen amusement of the hour.

It is not probable that candle-dipping bees were by any means a usual festivity in or very near New York city as late as the latter part of the eighteenth century. Rather should it be supposed that the evening at the Rhinelander mansion was a revival of an ancient custom, just as one occasionally hears in our day of some fashionable group of merrymakers holding a corn-husking bee in a barn

which may be finer than the dwellings of their
ancestors. Even so, it is a proof that when big
New York was little New Amsterdam, candle-
dipping had been one of its recognized festivities;
and it is for this reason that it is here introduced.

On this occasion each swain, as well as maiden,
was provided with a huge apron of checked linen,
and had full over-sleeves of the same material,
closed at the wrists and above the elbows by draw-
ing-strings, in order that no traces of soil might
afterward be found upon the silken hose and the
fine cloth knee-breeches of the young men, or on
the soft hanging, somewhat scanty folds of the
stuff gowns of the young women, or on the linen
ruffles and delicate laces which were worn alike by
both. At such industrial gatherings as this velvets and silks were worn by neither sex, but laces,
being washable, were permitted.

Thirty-two couples took part in that evening's
candle-dipping; and if my great-uncle's opinion
was trustworthy, all the girls were beautiful and
graceful, and all the youths were gallant and handsome. A portrait of Mr. Codwise when a young
man (taken by Earle) shows him as a very handsome, dark-eyed youth. I used often to look up
from the dear old face under an ugly wig, regarding me with such kindly eyes, to the bright-eyed,
curly-headed portrait on the wall, and could find
a trace of resemblance only in the lines of the
brow and the aquiline nose with its strong sug-

gestion of a terminating hook. In the eyes of
youth there is something incredible in so great a
change. To the dear old man, as he dwelt upon
the pleasures and companions of his youth, all of
them bore the same charms as in those happy
days. Unfortunately, I did not record their names,
but remember that there were Rutherfurds, Mor-
rises, Lawrences, Livingstons, Gracies, Stevenses,
Stuyvesants, Schuylers, Evertsons, Beeckmans,
Polhemuses, and Starrs among them, these names
being impressed by associations of one sort or another, while others have escaped my memory.

Of all who were present at this particular festival, "Gitty" (Gertrude) Rhinelander, the young
hostess, seemed to have been the sweetest and the
prettiest; and while the old gentleman always
smiled as he spoke of her, there was often a tear
in his faded eye while he sighed, "Poor Gitty!"
Why she was thus pitied as well as admired I ever
wondered, but had not the courage to inquire,
fancying always that she had met an early death,
and that a part of my good great-uncle's loyal
heart had been buried with her.

An evening of this sort of combined work and
fun began as early as six o'clock; and even so the
aprons and over-sleeves could not be doffed and
the supper begin much before ten o'clock. Substantial things were those Knickerbocker suppers!
Besides almost every seasonable variety of cold
fowl and game, there were cold roasts of beef and

spare-rib, and platters piled high with hot sausages and rollichies, while there was a great variety of pasties and boundless stores of sweetmeats and cake, placed all at once upon the big mahogany tables supported by many slender legs. Tea was never seen at late suppers, and coffee but rarely. Wines, principally Madeira, were plentifully served, though punch and egg-nog were the main reliance. General testimony seems to favor the tradition that while the Dutch were very generous providers of the wherewithal to make merry the hearts of the friends within their gates, neither they nor their guests of Dutch descent often became more than agreeably exhilarated. Mr. Codwise maintained that the same could not always be said of those of English, Scotch, or Irish birth or parentage.

After the supper came the dancing. There was no music save the fiddles of Castor and Pollux; but was that not enough? Have ever feet tripped more merrily than to the rollicking scrape of some inspired old wool-thatched fiddler, swaying to his own strains, and calling out the figures in clear, rich tones that harmonized with his wild dance measure as only his could do?

The closing dance, which always began at midnight, was perhaps brought from Holland by the first settlers. Mr. Codwise said that it was thought to be very old in his time, and considered to be the proper termination of festivities on all evening occasions. I am not aware of any existing description of it save his own, as I took it from his lips. It was called the "Fire Dance," and, if possible, was always "danced around a chimney."

In the Rhinelander house — which I imagine may have been the farmstead near the East River and the present Eighty-sixth Street and Second Avenue — there was then a central chimney-stack, which, on the ground floor, was triangular in shape. On one side of it the great kitchen and its pantries extended through the entire width of the house, the fireplace occupying the center of the inner wall. On the other side of the chimney the space was divided into two large connecting rooms, each having a fireplace across one corner. Any number of couples, from four upward, might engage in this dance, according to the capacity of the room. On this occasion there were sixteen couples in the kitchen and eight couples in each of the other rooms. The partners were arranged in rows opposite to each other in alternating vis-à-vis, so that when the gentleman of one couple faced his partner on the north, he of the next couple would face his partner on the south. The leading couple of each room advanced between the other dancers, bowing or courtesying, and swinging alternately each other and every other gentleman and lady in turn as they went on between the files of dancers, with many stately steps and flourishes the while.

The clasped right hands of the swinging couples were held as high as possible, the gentleman's left arm akimbo, and the lady's left hand holding her petticoats a little up, that her graceful steps and pretty ankles might be the better seen, until they reached the next room, where they became the " foot couple."

The dance lasted until each of the thirty-two couples had led in dancing round the chimney.

As each leading couple came opposite the fire-place in the room farthest from that in which they started, they courtesied and bowed and swung each other, reciting in Dutch some verses which were a sort of invocation to the spirit of friendship and good cheer. By this fireplace stood a tall and grinning Ganymede holding a very large tray filled with glasses of spiced punch — a beverage deemed to be a suitable preparation for a walk or a drive home over the snowy highways. After the invo-cation each lady was expected to taste and hand one of the glasses to her partner, while he — with-out tasting — handed her a smaller glass from the same tray.

All this while the steps and flourishes must not cease, and to succeed in draining the glasses with-out breaking the time-beat of the steps or spilling a drop of the liquor was the aim of each, a thing which could hardly have been achieved without sobriety and much previous practice. This practice all might easily attain, for traditions tell us that families of the better class among our Knickerbocker ancestors met at each other's houses almost every evening, save during the very longest days, for purposes of amusement, and that among amusements dancing held the first place. Children were allowed to take part during the first hour or two. A healthy, hearty, happy people they seem to have been, doing as much good and as little harm as may be in an imperfect world, leaving to their fortunate descendants fine examples of family affection, productive industry, broad charity, and placid content.

CHAPTER XXI

A MAN OF ENTERPRISE

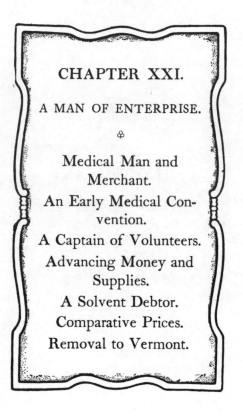

CHAPTER XXI.

A MAN OF ENTERPRISE.

☙

Medical Man and
Merchant.
An Early Medical Con-
vention.
A Captain of Volunteers.
Advancing Money and
Supplies.
A Solvent Debtor.
Comparative Prices.
Removal to Vermont.

YING in files in the old garret, carefully docketed, were several hundreds, perhaps more than a thousand, letters, all written in the same rather orderly-looking but very deceptive script; for it certainly is the most illegible hand I have ever undertaken to decipher, and my experience has not been small. In a prize contest it could no doubt hold its own against the worst chirography of Horace Greeley, or even that of Napoleon Bonaparte, which is usually conceded to be about on a par, for legibility, with the cuneiform characters of the Ninevites, in the eyes of the unlearned.

All these hundreds of old letters, stretching over a period of about fourteen years, were written by Simeon Smith, M.D., once of Sharon, Connecticut, but at the time that these were penned residing at Westhaven, Vermont.

Had the word been then invented, Dr. Smith would certainly have been known as a " hustler," for he was a man of boundless energy, versatility, and resource. As a physician he practically monopolized his immediate field, and was constantly called in consultation throughout a stretch of country ranging from the Hudson on the west to the Connecticut on the east, and for about twenty miles each way north and south from Sharon. Besides this, he was a soldier, a wholesale and retail merchant, a heavy dealer in real estate, and ever engaged in every local enterprise demanding energy, courage, capital, and public spirit.

Simeon Smith was a younger brother of the Rev. C. M. Smith, and, like the latter, was born in Suffield, Connecticut. He came to practise in Sharon about 1759, when he was twenty-three or twenty-four years old. At that period the colonies afforded little opportunity for gaining a thorough medical education, the usual way being for a young man to study with some elderly practitioner, whom he accompanied on his rounds, and for whom he ground, baked, and brewed the sometimes very queer decoctions which were prescribed for the unfortunate patients. How such a student got his degree I do not know. It is certain that comparatively few of those who then practised medicine in country places, and were styled "doctor," appear to have been entitled to write the consequential M.D. after their names.

It is probable that Dr. Smith received his medical education abroad; at least, his niece, our oft-quoted diarist Juliana, speaks of her "Uncle Simeon" as entertaining a Thanksgiving party with anecdotes of "his student days in Edinborough." Writing in 1802, Dr. Smith refers to a certain family event as having occurred when he "was in Edinborough in 1757," and there are traces extending through many years of a regular and for that day a frequent correspondence (that is to say, an exchange of letters as often as once or twice in two or three years) between Dr. Smith and two business firms, one in Edinburgh and one in London. From the first of these he received most of the new medical treatises as they appeared, and other books as well, for the doctor was evidently a lover of good literature; and from the second came surgical instruments, drugs, and all imaginable articles, from firearms to pins. In the letters from both of these parties there are references which would seem to prove the existence of a personal acquaintance, while there is no evidence to show that either of the foreign correspondents had ever been in America.

Almost as soon as Dr. Smith arrived in Sharon he established there a drug store which is believed to have been one of the largest and best of its kind in the "Old Thirteen." All the more important drugs were imported by Dr. Smith directly from London and Amsterdam, and were by him supplied to smaller dealers in many places, including New Haven, Hartford, Albany, and Poughkeepsie. The goods, of whatever sort, were first delivered in the original packages at the latter place, and from thence were distributed by Dr. Smith's agent. Each year preceding 1775 the number and variety of the country doctor's orders increased, still importing directly from London, Amsterdam, and various ports in the West Indies, until almost every salable thing that could be found anywhere in the colonies could be obtained from this quaint, old-fashioned country store, situated at such a distance from the centers of trade.

As a medical practitioner Dr. Smith was highly esteemed, though he did not prescribe as powerful doses as were then customary, and did not apply the lancet with the appalling frequency that was then habitual.

A subject which occupied much of Dr. Smith's thought for many years, though he was unable to carry out his plans, was the establishment of a school of medicine in his native State, which should be the equal of any in the New World. This project was not forgotten even during the stress of the War of the Revolution. In February, 1780, what was proudly announced as the " First Medical Society in The Thirteen United States of America since Their Independence " held a convention at Sharon by the invitation of Dr. Smith, the members being entertained principally at his house and those of his two brothers, the parson and " Deacon Paul." The establishment of such a school was a prominent topic before the convention, but nothing could be done to forward the execution of the plan, either then or for many years later, on account of the disturbed condition of finances all through the country.

In the old garret remains a copy of " AN ORA-TION ON THE RISE and PROGRESS of PHYSIC IN AMERICA, pronounced before the FIRST MEDICAL SOCIETY in the THIRTEEN UNITED STATES of AMERICA, since their INDEPENDENCE, At their CONVENTION held at SHARON, on the last Day of February, 1780." This was printed in Hartford, by Hudson & Goodwin, in 1781, in accordance with a vote of the aforesaid society.

In real estate Dr. Smith's transactions were, for his day, extensive, embracing large tracts in Dutchess and Columbia counties in New York, in Litchfield County, Connecticut, in Berkshire County, Massachusetts, in almost the whole line of western Vermont, and also in Canada. At the outbreak of the Revolution Dr. Smith's many pecuniary interests might be supposed to have rendered him likely to adopt the conservative side — that is, if there had been any truth in the allegation of the Tory party that the Whigs numbered in their ranks "only those who had nothing to lose." But the doctor was as active in politics as he was in everything else, and in 1776 he headed a company of Sharon men, who were with General Washington throughout his unfortunate Long Island campaign. This company was, with the exception of a few men who furnished their own outfits, equipped at Dr. Smith's expense. In 1777 he raised and partly equipped another company of volunteers to resist the advance of Burgoyne, but breaking his leg by an untimely accident, he was not able to head his company this time as he had done the previous year.

Dr. Smith never for one instant despaired of the ultimate success of our arms, and never hesitated to fill any orders for provisions, clothing, or medical stores sent to him from the State government, buying on his own personal security, which in his own region was more potent than that of the State, and taking the promissory notes of the State in compensation.

Dr. Smith's readiness to manifest his abiding faith in the eventual triumph of the revolting colonies had one result which, at the time and for a good many years afterward, caused him no little embarrassment.

In the struggling colony of Connecticut five thousand pounds had meant a very large sum of money even before the war; and during the war, before the Dutch loans and the French assistance had come to our financial aid, the value of such a sum was greater than ever. The State of Connecticut had voted to issue State bonds to what was then considered by many to be a rash amount. It is quite possible that the doctor had been one of those who had voted for this bond issue, for he represented his town in the Connecticut legislature for a good many sessions. If so, he was willing to give practical support to his vote, and had signified his readiness to take five thousand pounds, proposing to pay for the bonds in neat cattle or in other provision supplies for the troops. Gold and silver being at a premium, and Continental currency being at a very low valuation, this was but an extension of the prevailing system of barter.

His proposal to this effect was despatched by a messenger, who was expected to reach Hartford and return in about forty-eight hours, if nothing went amiss. But so much usually went amiss in even so short a journey as thirty or forty miles that no surprise would have been felt had the time been twice as long. The surprise came when, early in the morning of the second day, not the messenger, but two other men on horseback presented themselves at the wrought-iron gate before the big stone house, bringing a letter from Governor Trumbull to the effect that the horse of Dr. Smith's messenger having fallen lame, the governor had thought best to keep the man over for a day or two in Hartford, while, as the matter was urgent, he sent two confidential officials who were empowered to negotiate the whole affair with his friend the doctor.

The "confidential friends" explained that cash in hand—solid cash, golden guineas, or Spanish silver dollars — was the pressing need of the State, and to get this they were empowered to offer a considerable premium. Now, it so happened that the doctor had a neighbor — as neighbors were then counted; this one lived about five miles away — who had just inherited the accumulated stockingfuls of a miserly uncle. To this neighbor the doctor forthwith betook himself, and upon his personal note borrowed £3330, for which sum the governor's "friends" delivered a handsomely executed and duly signed State bond for £5000.

On the afternoon of the third day after his departure the doctor's own messenger returned with a sorry horse and a sorrier tale. To avoid the inconvenience of leaving this messenger without a designation we will call him X.

When X had reached Hartford he proceeded directly to the governor's office, where he was received by two men, who, after closely questioning him and reading the letter, as they said they had a right to do, being the governor's deputies, explained that the governor was out of town for a few days, but they could attend to everything during his absence. Meanwhile they treated X with a pleasing cordiality. Taking him to a certain tavern, which they assured him was the best in the country, they saw that he had a good supper and left him there to wait. This he did very willingly, waits of three or four days being the customary thing in the days when an absent person could only be summoned by a messenger on horseback. Poor X did not remember how or when he went to bed that night, but he was certain that he did not awake till a very late hour the next afternoon. When his head was finally clear enough to enable him to think about it, he went out to the stables, only to find that his fine horse had gone very lame. Taking him to a farrier was impossible, so the farrier was brought to the horse, and discovered that a long and rusty nail had been driven up into the horse's foot, causing a severe if not permanent injury. In the course of their talk X asked the farrier if he knew when the governor might be expected to return.

It then appeared that the governor had not been out of town at all. The farrier knew, because he had seen him every day, and sometimes three or four times a day, as he had to pass the governor's house on his way to and from his own.

Petty frauds were frequent enough in colonial and Revolutionary days, but frauds which might involve those who were nearly connected with affairs of state were not often heard of, and to the bucolic mind were almost inconceivable; yet something flickered through the poor messenger's brain. The lateness of the hour, his own condition, that of his horse, and the obvious lie told by the two *so* friendly clerks — perhaps all these things taken together might mean something? If so, that meaning could bode no good to his errand, though what shape the evil might take he could not guess.

Proceeding to the governor's house as speedily as he might, X found his Excellency already in a greatly perturbed state of mind. Two men who had long been employed by him in confidential business, and especially in business relating to the State bonds, had suddenly disappeared. They had been seen late on the previous evening, well mounted and carrying full saddle-bags, going westward. With them had also disappeared the entire issue of State bonds, lacking the governor's signature, but otherwise quite correct. Constables had been sent in pursuit, but the forgers had about sixteen hours the start of them, and in preëlectric days that was usually equivalent to an escape, especially as the constables had started on the theory that if the men were seen going westward they must have intended going in the opposite direction, and some of the pursuers had gone down the Connecticut River, and some had turned northward.

After many a long day — not until about 1794, in fact — one of the forgers was apprehended and brought back to Connecticut for trial, but what the result was the old letters do not inform us. Two other would-be supporters of the State's finances, in addition to Dr. Smith, had been victimized before the forgeries had become known, but neither of the two rendered any aid to the doctor or the State in their persistent pursuit of the criminals. In the end only one was apprehended. He was discovered among the refugee Tories in New Brunswick by Dr. Smith himself, while on a prospecting tour he was making, on the outlook for mines of coal or of iron ore.

The forgeries were said to have been singularly perfect. Dr. Smith was well acquainted with the handwriting of Governor Trumbull, and the forged letter, when compared with the undoubted letters of the governor which Dr. Smith had received at various times, though it might have excited the suspicions of a modern chirographic expert, was acknowledged by the governor to be perfect enough to have deceived himself. For a time the existence of these forged bonds caused much perplexity to the State government, and would have caused still more had intelligence concerning them been published through the length and breadth of the land, as it would now be. There were a few advantages to be derived from the slow methods of the time.

In mines of every description Dr. Smith was always interested. When buying real estate he always had a clause inserted granting to his ownership all the mines thereon, "whether opened or yet to be discovered," and whenever he sold any land, let the same be much or little, all such rights were expressly reserved by him. His Edinburgh correspondent had standing orders always to send him any new book of importance concerning mines and their workings. Some of these, both in Latin and in English, still remain in the old home, and probably there are others at his fine Vermont residence. But I do not know that any appreciable part of the two fortunes which the doctor made came from his mining ventures.

By the close of the Revolutionary War, when he had time to think about it, Dr. Smith found that, to use a modernism, he had " expanded too much." The times were hard, very, very hard, for all. The Continental money had fallen so low as to be practically worthless. Gold and silver had almost disappeared. Barter took the place of coin, and when a debt could not be paid in produce or in goods, then there was the debtors' prison; and into that most illogical of all legal devices must the honestest of debtors helplessly fall if his creditors were pressing.

The illiberal, unjust, and unwise system of imprisonment for debt was about as disastrous in its results upon the creditors as upon the debtors, but it was an astonishing number of years before any appreciable number of the former seem to have perceived this fact.

To show the operation of the generally depressed state of finances, it may be well to quote some of the prices brought by imported articles, and the proportionately small rates received for articles of home production, as shown by Dr. Smith's account-books for 1785-90, the items being taken at random.

Beef, by the quarter, brought one cent per pound; sewing-silk was sold at "six pence *per yard*." A pound of sugar was "two shillings thripence"; a bushel of oats was "two shillings sixpence." Five hundred feet of pine boards brought one pound two shillings and sixpence, and two "Bandanna" handkerchiefs were worth as much. But the worst state of things is shown by the price, or rather the no-price, of the Continental currency, six hundred and sixty-nine Continental dollars being exchanged (in 1785) for only five pounds and four cents of what was known in Connecticut as "York State money," which was rated at about half the value of the pound sterling. As paper money was so nearly valueless, the gold and silver coins of foreign nations were employed when barter would not suffice. This must have added greatly to the difficulties of business. In 1794 the sum of one hundred and thirty pounds and some shillings was paid in "pistoles," "pieces johannis," Spanish dollars, guineas, and three New York bank bills, the latter at a considerable discount. Each piece of the gold was weighed separately and no two of the same nominal value were rated alike.

The demands made against Dr. Smith grew more and more urgent, but, full of resources as he was, he kept on satisfying them until at last, four years after the close of the war, he was obliged to realize that there was no relief in the near future,

and that without putting himself beyond the juris-
diction of his State he would eventually find himself at the mercy of some narrow-minded creditor
who could put his debtor in a place where the
most resourceful of living men would find himself
as helpless as the dead Julius Cæsar.

Summoning his brother, the Rev. C. M. Smith,
and the latter's son (the "brother Jack" of the
diary), then a stripling lawyer of twenty-two years,
the doctor laid his case before them, and also his
plans to retrieve his fortunes. He made over to
his brother the larger and more valuable parts of
his property in and about Sharon, on the condition
that his brother should satisfy all the most pressing
of his debts. By realizing upon the more immediately salable portions of the doctor's property, as
well as of his own and that of his wife, the parson,
after a time, was able to accomplish this. As usual,
the biggest creditors were the least pressing. The
man who had furnished the £3330 to buy the
forged note, having always received his interest
with regularity, was present at this interview of
the brothers, and would not accept of any security
for the amount which was still due him; but this
was eventually paid, together with all the other
debts, in full.

Besides a good many farms and other odd bits
of real estate scattered through three States, the
doctor still possessed about twenty-five thousand
acres of land in the then territory of Vermont;

and thither he and his wife wended their toilsome way. It is at this point that his many letters begin. The new State needed countless things, and the doctor was the man to supply them. In every letter there is a demand for this, that, or the other thing that is "absolutely necessary and must be sent forthwith." Herds of cattle, unnumbered yokes of oxen,— "because they can travel these trackless wilds better than horses,"— wagons, cart wheels, sleds, "tools for a wheelright and a man to use them," a "farrier and all the tools for his trade," "machinery for a sawmill of the biggest kind," a "linnen and a woollen loom and a weaver for each of them, good ones who understand their trade," were among the things sent for, while his old correspondents in Great Britain, Holland, and the West Indies forwarded to his new abode and his new store all the things which they had been wont to supply to his first.

In Vermont all of the doctor's enterprises prospered, and as rapidly as possible both principal and interest of all the debts which he had left behind were repaid; and when he wrote his last letter to "Dear Johnny," a month or two before his death, in 1804, he was able to say:

"At last I owe no man on earth a penny that cannot be paid at a moment's notice, and I now have leisure to devote to my favorite project,— the establishment in my native State of as fine a

Medical College and *Hospital* connected therewith as may be in any Country. I am not yet seventy, my health is good. I hope to live to see it started. In my time *Great Things* have happened and *greater* are to come. I wish I could live a Thousand Years! I suppose your Father will shake his head over this, but I believe the Lord has a great work for this Country to do, and *I want to see it!*"

In spite of this desire and his good health, the brave old doctor had not reached seventy years when he calmly fell asleep. All his worldly affairs were in good condition, and he left to his widow and to his favorite nephew what, for his day, was considered the large fortune of something over one hundred thousand dollars.

CHAPTER XXII

A COUNTRY PARSON'S USEFUL LIFE

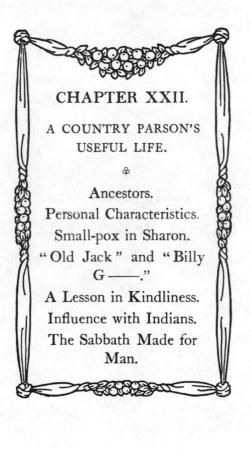

CHAPTER XXII.

A COUNTRY PARSON'S USEFUL LIFE.

☙

Ancestors.
Personal Characteristics.
Small-pox in Sharon.
"Old Jack" and "Billy
G———."
A Lesson in Kindliness.
Influence with Indians.
The Sabbath Made for
Man.

HE Rev. Cotton Mather Smith was a member of what the "Autocrat of the Breakfast Table" and Richard Grant White used to delight in calling the Brahman class of New England, meaning the descendants of the early ministers and magistrates of the Plymouth, Massachusetts, and Connecticut colonies.

The ministers from whom he was descended were the Rev. Henry Smith of Wethersfield, and the Rev. Richard Mather of Dorchester, while he was collaterally related to all the "preaching Mathers," and to the Rev. John Cotton of Boston. Mr. Smith's father, grandfather, and great-grandfather of his own surname all fought in the numerous colonial wars. A colonial governor and a major-general were numbered among his ancestors, besides many magistrates and officers of lesser rank. Hence it is not wonderful that while Mr. Smith was a man of peace he was also in favor of fighting in a good cause.

The Rev. A. R. Robbins of Norfolk, Connecticut, who was for many years the beloved pastor of the Congregational church in that place, was a lifelong friend of Mr. Smith's, never allowing a year to pass without an exchange of visits, though this was not an easy matter with the twenty miles of steep hills intervening. A son of the former, the Rev. Thomas Robbins of Hartford, Connecticut, well remembered his father's friend, and writing in 1850 said:

"The Rev. Cotton Mather Smith was minister of a parish in the immediate neighborhood of my father's (Norfolk, Connecticut), and was often a visitor at our house in my early years. My personal acquaintance with him was chiefly in that period. . . . Mr. Smith was rather tall . . . and united great benignity and acute intelligence in his expression. His manners were remarkably polished, so that he might have appeared to advantage even in a Court; they were a delightful compound of simplicity, grace and dignity; while on the other hand they were entirely free from hauteur or ostentation, and he could make the humblest man in the community feel at home in his company. . . . He never performed an act or uttered a word that was fitted needlessly to wound others or to lessen the influence of his own fine character. . . . He had a good deal of unction in the pulpit, but his manner was simple, natural and graceful."

The sermons of that time were usually written

out in full, and read in a more or less pleasing manner; but though the outlines of Mr. Smith's sermons were carefully thought out in the study, he trusted to the inspiration of the moment for the dress in which he offered them to his congregation. Many instances of his eloquence are still traditionally related. As it is a matter of record that the church of the Sharon pastor was twice enlarged during his ministry to accommodate the increasing numbers of his hearers, and that persons residing in parishes from ten to twenty-five miles distant from his own were among the frequent attendants at his ministrations, it is probable that his confidence in the inspiration of the moment was well founded.

Though Mr. Smith's fame as an eloquent preacher was locally great, it was as a pastor that he was longest remembered.

In my girlhood there were still many old persons who had known him, and the mingled feeling of reverence and affection with which they mentioned his name was pleasant to know. The anecdotes were many, showing him in many lights. Some persons told how, "during the awful small-pox winter, when the weather was as cold as was ever known in New England, he and his heroic wife banished themselves for three months from their own house, taking refuge in an outbuilding, where their indispensable wants were supplied by an old slave who had had the dreaded disease, that they might be free to come and go while ministering to the sick and dying, without endangering the neighbors or their own household." This was related to me by a very old lady — Mrs. Deming, mother of the late Dr. Ralph Deming, a "beloved physician" of Sharon, who died in 1877. "It was no wonder that all loved Parson Smith," said the old lady. "He was the good shepherd who was always ready to lay down his life for his flock."

Another has recorded that "this visitation of the smallpox put all Mr. Smith's benevolence, contrivance, activity and fortitude in requisition. . . . For nineteen successive days and nights the humble imitator of Him who went about healing all manner of sickness and all manner of disease among the people, put not off his clothes for rest." Mr. Smith was possessed of no little medical skill, and it was always freely at the service of any who required it.

An instance which shows the parson's sense of humor, combined with a gentle and kindly dignity, was told by my grandfather, who himself strongly resembled his grandfather in these and other qualities. Among the orphans, several of whom were always sheltered and cared for in the parsonage, was one young incorrigible who, by way of punishment for some fault, was one fine Sunday in June forbidden to attend morning service. This might not, nowadays, be deemed a severe chastisement, but then the Sundays gave the one opportunity of the week for social intercourse.

While the sermon was in progress, presumably to the satisfaction of all present in the old meetinghouse, there was a movement among the boys who filled the first gallery, and an irresistible but half-smothered chuckle ran around among them, as fire runs through stubble. The second or topmost gallery, where the slaves sat, was in a still more visible and audible commotion. Even the decorous tenants of the big square pews on the ground floor seemed to find some difficulty in following the thread of the parson's discourse. The parson redoubled his efforts, and at the same time the commotion in the auditory was increasing.

The preacher stopped and looked around with some displeasure, but more wonder. Every one was looking in his direction, and yet no one was looking at him. His wife was biting her lips with a vexation belied by her laughing eyes.

The old slave Jack could stand it no longer. Making his way behind the seats crowded by his brethren, whose ivories were unusually exposed, to the end of the topmost gallery, which was that in which he presided as the self-constituted maintainer of discipline among his own race, Jack stepped forth upon the flat top of the massive soundingboard, which was on a level with this gallery floor and hung like a threatening extinguisher above the pulpit. Here he was for a moment in full

view of the congregation, but hidden from the
parson's sight, until he reappeared returning to his
own seat, and bearing in his arms a very happy and
complacent black-and-tan dog, which had been
decorated by a pair of the parson's best bands, and
then released from the durance in which he always
had to be kept on Sunday to prevent him from following his master to church. The eager Carlo had
found that he could not get in by the doors from
the vestibule into the body of the meeting-house,
or even by those of the first gallery, so he had ascended the stairs leading to the top gallery, and
then had reached the sounding-board, on which he
had been gravely seated, apparently well pleased
with himself and his ministerial garb, and, to those
who had perceptions of the ludicrous, seemed to
be mocking his unconscious master in the pulpit
beneath.

As Jack reappeared bearing the unresisting dog,
— for Carlo was a faithful friend, and cultivated no
color prejudices,— the aggrieved old slave turned
toward his master, breaking all meeting-house rules
by exclaiming, with irrepressible indignation:
" Massa, massa ! Dis some mo' o' dat Bill G——'s
debiltry. He got 'o be stop' *somehow !* "

This was too much. From the pulpit along the
crowded seats of the two galleries even to the decorous depths of the deacons' pew on the main
floor, a laughter that was more than rippling was
both seen and heard, clearly to the scandal of the

frowning and belligerent Jack, and perhaps to that of some of the severer magnates of the pews. But what would you? The pranks as well as the misfortunes of the mischievous Billy G—— were well known but always unexpected to the little community; and the sense of humor is one which has seldom been denied to kindly natured folk. The parson was never troubled about his own dignity, probably feeling it too firm to need protection, so he laughed with the rest, while gently bidding Jack to relieve the dog of his offending finery and take him home. Then, turning to the congregation, he said that the little boy's jest had been made without any malicious intent, and without a sense of the disrespect it would be showing to the Lord's house. The child, he said, was too young to realize this, and "as we would have our own sins of either wilfulness or ignorance pardoned by our Heavenly Father, so must we pardon the offenses of children, and especially those of the fatherless." From this he talked on, dwelling upon the duties of all members of Christ's church toward the younger and weaker of the flock, until, after the benediction, "his hearers could only greet each other silently for the tender emotions which filled their hearts."

Neither public nor private admonition was given to the delinquent Billy (save possibly by old Jack in the barn), and the flow of his jokes did not cease, though after this they were of a less public character. In later years he went to South Carolina, and there became a physician of some local reputation, though dying before reaching the prime of life. Recognizing his approaching end, he left to Parson Smith the care of his two motherless children and their little inheritance — a sure proof of the confidence he had retained in the faithful kindness of the friend who had pardoned so many of his own boyish offenses.

Indeed, Mr. Smith ever possessed a certain boyishness of heart which, from his earliest years to his latest, gave him great influence over the young of all classes. While still a college student he was associated with Dr. Jonathan Edwards in the charge of a school which had been established among the Indians at Stockbridge, Massachusetts. Here were early brought into play the same powers of intellect and the generous qualities of heart which distinguished him through life.

His influence over his wild pupils, which was great, was first gained by his agility, strength, and skill in all athletic sports, especially in marksmanship, in leaping and in running, in which things it is stated that he easily excelled all his white competitors and most Indians. The Indians could well appreciate the young minister's superiority in a line so peculiarly their own, and the influence it gained over them was increased and retained by the unfailing justice and perfect courtesy which characterized all his dealings with them. "At the same time," says Dr. Sprague, in his "Annals of the American Pulpit," "he labored for and with them with untiring diligence and corresponding success, and became a proficient in their language while imparting to them his own."

Twenty years after Mr. Smith's labors in Stockbridge had ended, two of his former Indian pupils accompanied Colonel Hinman's regiment on its trying march through the wilderness to Fort Ticonderoga. During the dangerous illness there of their former teacher and then chaplain, these Indians devoted themselves to his service, and that of his wife after her arrival, with a touching assiduity. On his return to Sharon they helped to bear his litter for the journey, which consumed nearly two weeks, although burdens of any kind were usually despised by their race ; and for many years thereafter they paid him an annual visit. They always spoke with great pride of their quondam teacher's youthful athletic accomplishments, although similar gifts were not then so unusual in the clerical profession as they afterward became.

In Mr. Smith's time all country ministers were, by force of circumstances rather than choice, both farmers and huntsmen; and sometimes they were carpenters and smiths as well, and saw nothing incongruous in their diverse employments. Certainly their congregations must have been the gainers by the exercise which made their spiritual head so physically robust, the health of the mind depending so much upon that of the body.

As an army chaplain Mr. Smith seems to have been very successful in a more than usually difficult

situation.   General Schuyler, one of the best officers
and most honorable men of our Revolutionary War,
highly esteemed by General Washington and other
officers whose good opinions were medals of honor,
was heartily disliked by the New England troops.
The reason for this dislike is well explained by Mrs.
Smith in her account of her journey to join her husband at Ticonderoga.   She says:

"My Husband, as Chaplain, had used his influence with the men to soften the bitterness of feeling
which so many of them entertained toward the
'Dutchman,' as they were wont somewhat con-
temptuously to style General Schuyler. The latter
is a man of the purest patriotism and of much
ability, but he was then unused to the state of
things in our Colonies of New England, whereby
a man of the best birth and breeding may yet be a
mechanic or a tradesman by reason of the poverty
of the land, and the fact that so many of our fore-
fathers had been obliged to give up all their estates when for conscience sake they left the Mother
Country. On the contrary such of the settlers from
Holland as were of good family were able to bring
their worldly goods with them to the new land and
by reason of the fertility of the soil and their advan-
tageous trade with the Indians were never obliged
to resort to handicrafts for a livelihood.

"My Husband has many times told me of the
surprise of General Schuyler to find that one of our

Trained Band Men whom he knew to be but a carpenter, was at the same time a man of much influence and an office holder in his native town, being the son of a magistrate appointed by the Crown. He could never be brought to see that while we in Connecticut were all so much on a social equality, it was yet an equality on a high plane; while on the other hand it was difficult for our men (so many of whom, though poor, had received the best education the country afforded) not to feel themselves superior to 'a parcel of stupid Dutchmen', (thus discourteously, I grieve to say, were they often referred to), many of whom spoke but imperfect English and almost none of whom had received a college training. My Husband had always been striving to bring about a better understanding between the troops of Connecticut and those of New York, and had thus gained and still retains the active friendship of General Schuyler, while he was always much liked as well as reverenced by all the soldiers in the command."

The Rev. Dr. McEwing of New London, Connecticut, writing in 1855, when there were still living many old people who remembered Mr. Smith, says:

"The American Revolution found Mr. Smith in the maturity of his powers, wielding, within his sphere, a great influence. He had dedicated himself to the Christian ministry, but this did not make him too sacred to give himself to his country. His brethren, the Congregational clergymen of New England, were, at large, distinguished patriots in the struggle for independence. None of them in the incipient movements of the Revolution, or in providing for the hardships and conflicts of the War, brought the people of their charges up to a higher tone of action than did the Pastor of Sharon. His sermons, his prayers, the hymns he gave to the choir, were impulsive to patriotism, . . . but domestic action did not satisfy him. Into the momentous campaign of 1775 he entered as chaplain to a regiment in the Northern Army. His influence in producing good order and cultivating morals in the camp, in consoling the sick " (and, it might be added, in taking care of them), " and in inspiring the army with firmness and intrepidity attracted the admiration of all."

In Sedgwick's " History of Sharon " it is stated :

" Parson Smith, like the other clergymen of the day, was a most ardent and decided Whig, and his personal influence contributed not a little to lead the public mind in the right channel. . . . The intelligence of the battle of Lexington was brought to Sharon on the Sabbath, and Mr. Smith at the close of the morning exercises, announced it from the pulpit and made some remarks tending to arouse the spirit of the people to firmness and resistance. Immediately after the congregation was dismissed, the militia and volunteers, to the number of one hundred men, paraded on the west side of the street, south of the meeting-house and prepared to march immediately to the scene of action."

After Mr. Smith's enforced return from the fighting field he still continued his active work of inspiring the soldiers, keeping the home-stayers up to their duty as providers for those in the field, and comforting those who had sent, and sometimes those who had lost, their best beloved.

In still more practical ways was manifested the parson's earnestness in the cause. During this war the only sources of food-supply were to be found in the unharassed portions of the thirteen States, and it was as essential that every possible spear of grain or hill of corn should be raised to supply provisions for the army as it was to furnish the men and ammunition.

During the early part of one week in the summer of 1779 a very large quantity of wheat had been cut by the Sharon farmers, and bound into sheaves, and these, in view of threatening rain, not being sufficiently cured to put into the barns, had been piled into shocks in such a way as to shed the rain if it did not prove to be of too penetrating a quality. But this it proved to be, and the hearts of all grew heavier and heavier, for the continued wet was a menace of "sprouted wheat," from which wholesome flour could not be made.

Thursday, Friday, Saturday, the rain poured down upon the wheat-fields, of which more had been sown than ever before in the history of the township, owing to the country's pressing needs, and the crops per acre were greater than ever before, as the early part of the season had been favorable in that vicinity.

On Saturday, at sunset, the rain was still steadily descending, but on the Sunday morning the sun rose brilliantly. According to the creed of the weather-wise, any change in the weather that could be depended upon to last for more than twenty-four hours must take place in the daytime. It was plain to the dullest that another rain upon the wheat would leave it in a hopeless condition.

Yet, with few exceptions, the farmers all assembled at the meeting-house on the Sabbath morning, filled with gravest apprehensions concerning the fate of the precious wheat, and at the same time showing a grim determination to lose it, if needs must, rather than to do wrong.

The people usually mustered at the church a good while before the stated service time, while the parson was always punctual at the moment. On this day he was descried approaching the meeting-house at an even more rapid pace than usual, and a full half-hour earlier, and not accompanied by his family or near neighbors.

Hastily mounting the southern flight of exterior steps, and standing there, the parson announced that there would be no sermons preached by him that day. The wheat was in danger, and, in the great struggle in which they were engaged, wheat meant human lives. As the Sabbath was made for man, it was plain that to save lives on that day was a proper Sabbatical labor. He then, still standing at the top of the steps, offered a very short prayer, and dismissed the congregation with a benediction, and an exhortation to all who had no endangered wheat of their own to give their services to those who needed them most.

So numerous were the laborers, so well and rapidly did they all work, so briskly blew the drying wind, and so hotly shone the harvest sun, that by the time the night dews had begun to gather the crop had been saved.

In this labor the women and even the children had borne their share ; for they could toss up the wet wheat-spears by forkfuls to catch the wind and sun as well as could the men. Very early in the morning the parson had sent his household into his own fields, and had advised all of his near-by neighbors of his opinion in regard to the duty of the moment.

His daughter Juliana, writing of this unwonted Sabbath-day employment, says:

" Papa, Mamma, Sister Betsey, Brothers Jack and Tommy and I all worked as hard as we could all day, not only in our wheat, but in that of Uncle Simeon and Uncle Paul after ours was all done."

Such an instance is worth recording, because it is by no means likely that it was the only one of its kind, though so much has been said about the ultra-strictness of the Puritans. They certainly did not approve of " needless labors or vain recreations on the Lord's Day," but I think it will be found that they believed in doing whatever was necessary to forward the undertakings which seemed righteous in their eyes on any day of the week.

CHAPTER XXIII

"WELL DONE, GOOD AND FAITHFUL"

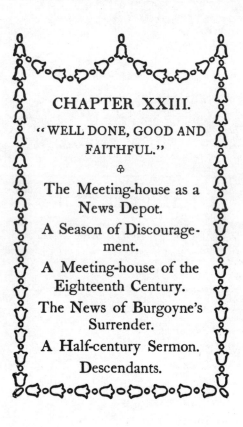

CHAPTER XXIII.

"WELL DONE, GOOD AND
FAITHFUL."

♣

The Meeting-house as a
News Depot.

A Season of Discourage-
ment.

A Meeting-house of the
Eighteenth Century.

The News of Burgoyne's
Surrender.

A Half-century Sermon.

Descendants.

ROM the earliest days the meeting-house was the place to hear, and the minister was the person to announce, all political news of importance. During the Revolutionary War there was an ever-growing anxiety to hear from the distant "front,"— so very distant it was in those days of toilsome communication!— and on Sunday mornings, fully an hour before service time, people would begin to gather around the meeting-house from every direction; for it was here, if anywhere, that private news from the army might be met. Opportunities for sending letters home were few; but sometimes a packet might be received that had passed from hand to hand. A might have happened to be coming from the Army of the North down as far as Albany, and there have given the packet to B, who chanced to have business in Red Hook, at which place he found that C was going to Poughkeepsie, whence the latter's friend D might be called to go to Pleasant Valley, and there find E ready to convey the precious missive to the waiting friends in Sharon, who considered intelligence less than a fortnight old as fresh news.

In the autumn of 1777 it was many weeks since one of these rare bundles of letters from the Northern army had reached Sharon. Sad to sternness were the faces which gathered about the high steps of the meeting-house on a certain bright October morning.

For a long time everything had seemed to be going against the revolting colonies. They had lost New York, Newport, Ticonderoga, and Philadelphia, had suffered wasting defeats on Long Island and at Fort Washington, and been badly beaten at Brandywine and Germantown. To offset these losses were only the victory at Trenton and the partial success at Princeton. The British controlled the Lower Hudson, and made destructive raids upon southern Connecticut, marking their course by the ashes of defenseless towns and the blood of non-combatants.

On the north the advance of Burgoyne had been nearly unchecked. On the west, in the State of New York, lay the notoriously Royalist county of Dutchess. Thus this part of western Connecticut seemed to lie between three fires, and, unprotected as it was left because nearly all its able-bodied men were in Gates's army, it had many and grave reasons for apprehension. When the eyes of one met those of another, there was an unuttered question in every glance.

While the near-by members of the congregation

came on foot, probably most of those from a distance arrived on horseback. The meeting-house itself I can delineate from the descriptions given me by my father, Robert Worthington Smith, who remembered it well, as it was not taken down until 1824, having been used for sixty-one years. The house was about eighty feet by sixty in dimensions, and stood about midway in the broad street, and nearly in front of the present edifice, upon a somewhat steep pitch of rocks which has since been blasted away and filled in, so that only a gentle green slope remains.

The house had three doors of entrance, each reached by long flights of stairs on the north, east, and south sides. The greatest length of the meeting-house was from north to south, but the three main aisles, one quite broad and the other two narrower, ran from east to west, while short cross-aisles connected the north and south doors with the main side aisles. On the west side, reached by a flight of steps some sixteen feet in height, was the lofty pulpit, overhung by the cumbrous extinguisher-like sounding-board. The square pews were divided into three groups, the middle group being for families, that on the south side for maidens who had no family ties and did not belong to the choir, and for widows; that on the north side was reserved for single men who did not sing. The front pews of the central group were considered the posts of honor.

Around three sides of the building ran high galleries, the lower one opposite the pulpit containing the choir. Starting from the center of the choir, the bass and counter-singers tapered off toward the north side gallery, where sat the taller boys nearest the choir, and after them the smaller boys nearer to the pulpit. Starting again from the middle of the choir and going south, the " air " and " second " singers (wearing funny little close, white caps instead of the big bonnets, which were supposed to, and probably did, break the volume of the wearers' voices) shaded off by soft gradations to young girls who held hymn-books and tried to appear unconscious of the fact that there were boys (with eyes) in the opposite gallery. Over the first ran a second but narrower gallery, set apart, the one side for the male and the other for the female slaves.

Into the church which was built in 1824, near to the old one, stoves were immediately placed; but in that in which Parson Smith preached no such comfort was known. This building was finished in 1768, and though there were no fireplaces, the danger of setting fire to their new church by means of the foot-stoves began immediately to exercise the minds of the church-members, and a fine of ten shillings was exacted for each foot-stove that might be carelessly left within the church after the hours of service.

At the last stroke of the bell, on a certain Sunday of late October in 1777, a quick, emphatic footfall rang on the stone step leading from the ground to the southern entrance, and all in the building rose, not so much to show their deference to the pastor whom they all loved as to manifest their reverence to the ordained servant of their common Master. As the preacher came down the aisle he gravely and graciously acknowledged the bows and courtesies of the people in the pews. After ascending the stairs to the pulpit, he paused a moment to bow to the front, then to the right, and then to the left. This was the signal that all might now be seated, and in the general soft rustle that ensued the pastor waited with bowed head.

On this day both prayers and hymns seemed prophetic — at least, every person who told of it long after always said so. When the text was announced, "Watchman, what of the night? The watchman saith, The morning cometh," its last three words rang out with such a clarion tone that all present felt that this was to be "a field day with the Parson." Earnest sometimes to vehemence, gifted with a melodious and powerful voice, and glowing with natural eloquence, Mr. Smith's sermons never lacked originality and force, and on this day his flock thought him inspired as with faithful stroke he drew the picture of an oppressed people struggling for liberty against fearful odds. Tears coursed unrestrained down cheeks better accustomed to the touch of snow and wind, as the late reverses were recounted, until some of the older members began to wonder "what Parson could be thinking of, to discourage the people so?" Then suddenly his tone changed. "Our weakness," he said, "is the Lord's opportunity. He has permitted our past humiliation that our sins might be punished and that He might show us that He is mighty to save. He has promised to succor those who look to Him for their help, and He is faithful who has promised." Then, kindling as with prophetic fire, his face glowing, his lithe form dilating and quivering with feeling, he triumphantly exclaimed:

"Behold! the morning NOW cometh. I see its beams already gilding the mountain tops. Its brightness is already bursting over all the land." He closed his Bible and stood with uplifted hand, while a silence, as of expectation, fell alike upon the preacher and his hearers. Then, during the solemn hush which preceded the benediction, could be distinguished from afar the hasty clatter of a horseman dashing into the village from the north. Faces turn toward the doors, but not a whisper breaks the hush. All know that the sacred stillness of a New England Sabbath would not be thus broken without good reason. The eager horseman makes directly for the church. Hope is triumphant over fear, but with hope is mingled terror, and anxious eyes blaze out from blanched faces as the rider, springing from his horse, enters the church, his spurs clanking along the uncarpeted floor and up the pulpit stairs.

The parson, his face flushing with the joy of a hope fulfilled, read only the three words, "Burgoyne has surrendered," and then burst into honorable tears. The next moment, calmed and solemn, he said, "Let us thank God for this great mercy." And moved by a common impulse, the whole congregation rose to the Puritan posture of prayer — the erect posture of the Ironsides, who prayed and fought and kept their powder dry; and stern and self-contained as they were, they thought it no shame to shed tears of thankfulness.

I have heard this story so often, not from those who had been present, of course, but from those whose parents had related it to them, that I can hardly realize that I, too, was not there to feel the haunting anxiety, the thrilling hope, the over-whelming joy of that glorious news.

The country parson's duties in colonial days embraced all that a similar charge now implies, and some that the modern minister knows nothing of. He was in all things expected to be the leader of his people. They looked to him for example in things political, social, and educational as well as in things theological, and it must in common justice be said that the pastor who failed to fulfil these expectations to the best of his ability was rarely found.

His duties were so many and so diverse that it was well that he had not also to contend with the rush, hurry, and consequent pressure of our own time. He had to work with hands as well as head, but he had not to compete with brilliant minds all over the continent whose Sunday utterances could be read at the Monday morning breakfast-tables of his deacons and elders, and compared with his own. Each pastor had the sick, the poor, the vicious, and the uncultured of his own small field to care for and struggle to bring to better circumstances and to higher ideals; but he did not have to concern himself about similar conditions and responsibilities all over the world; and if he did not seem to accomplish all that the same man would do in these days, he perhaps left a deeper impression on the minds of those among whom he lived and labored. The very long pastorates of that time would be almost a physical impossibility now.

There then existed no prejudice to long periods of candidacy. It was felt that the relation between pastor and flock should be, as it generally was, permanent, and should not be entered upon without due deliberation. Mr. Smith preached in Sharon as a candidate for more than a year, and was finally ordained pastor in August, 1755. In 1805 he preached his half-century sermon from the text: "Now lettest thou thy servant depart in peace: . . . for mine eyes have seen thy salvation" (Luke ii. 29, 30).

After this Mr. Smith survived but little more than a year, dying in November, 1806. His greatly lamented wife had died six years before

while in Albany, visiting her daughter, Mrs.
Radcliff.

Thomas, the elder son of the Rev. and Mrs.
Cotton Mather Smith, died at the age of nineteen.
Elizabeth, their eldest daughter, married Dr. Lem-
uel Wheeler, a surgeon at one time attached to
General Washington's command, and afterward
practising at Red Hook, now Tivoli, New York.
Mrs. Wheeler left two daughters, one of whom
became the wife of the Hon. John Davenport of
New Haven, Connecticut, and the other was married to Mr. Hubert Van Waganen of Poughkeepsie, New York.

The youngest daughter, Mary, married the Rev.
Daniel Smith, for many years the pastor of the
Congregational Church of Stamford, Connecticut.
Years after the latter's decease it was discovered
that he also was descended from the Rev. Henry
Smith of Wethersfield. She left a son and daugh-
ter. The first became the Rev. Thomas Mather
Smith, for many years the head of the Theological
Seminary at Gambier, Ohio. He was father of
the Rev. John Cotton Smith, D.D., for more than
twenty years the much-loved rector of the Church
of the Ascension in New York city, dying in 1882.
The sister of the Rev. T. M. Smith married Milo
L. North, M.D., an eminent physician of Hartford,
Connecticut, and Saratoga, New York.

Juliana, the diarist to whom we are so much in-
debted, married, as before stated, the Hon. Jacob

Radcliff, a member of the Supreme Court of Judicature of the State of New York, and for three terms mayor of New York city. Mrs. Radcliff died in 1823, leaving two daughters. The elder of these, Maria, married Mr. W. Tillman of Troy, New York, while the younger, Julia, married an English gentleman named Spencer, who settled in Elizabeth, New Jersey.

From all of Parson Smith's three daughters have descended noble, strong, and sweet men and women. The only one of his sons who survived to an adult age was John Cotton Smith, who early entered political life and left it only with the disruption of the Federal party, to which he was attached. He was the last Federal governor of his State, retiring in 1817 — "the most popular man of an unpopular party," says S. G. Goodrich, in his "Recollections." The correspondence between Parson Smith and this son, extending at intervals from 1779 to 1806, is a beautiful record of paternal and filial affection. From those closely written foolscap sheets of coarse but excellent linen paper have been gleaned many of the facts relating to domestic life which have been inserted in these pages.